THE
CRITICAL SENSE

OTHER BOOKS BY JAMES REEVES

ANTHOLOGIES

Heinemann's Junior Poetry Books: a collection of rhymes and poems for use in Primary Schools
1 *Yellow Wheels*   2 *Grey Goose and Gander*
3 *Green Broom*   4 *Strawberry Fair*
The Merry-Go-Round (the above four books in one volume)
The Rhyming River, I–IV (four books for Secondary Schools)
Orpheus Book I (English poetry for 10–12-year-olds)
Orpheus Book II (English poetry for 13–15-year-olds)
The Poets' World (an anthology of English Poetry)
The Speaking Oak (a miscellany of English prose and poetry)
Dialogue and Drama (a dramatic anthology) with Norman Culpan
The Idiom of the People (folk-song texts from the Mss. of Cecil Sharp)
The Everlasting Circle (folk-song texts from the Mss. of S. Baring-Gould, H. E. D. Hammond and George B. Gardiner)
A New Canon of English Poetry with M. Seymour-Smith

LITERARY CRITICISM

A Short History of English Poetry
Understanding Poetry

PLAYS FOR YOUNG PLAYERS

Mulcaster Market
The King who took Sunshine

POEMS FOR CHILDREN

Hurdy-Gurdy
The Wandering Moon
Prefabulous Animiles with Edward Ardizzone

THE POETRY BOOKSHELF SERIES

Selections with introduction, notes and portraits

D. H. Lawrence   *Emily Dickinson*
John Donne   *Samuel Taylor Coleridge*
Gerard Manley Hopkins   *Robert Browning*
John Clare   *The Modern Poets' World*
Jonathan Swift   *Andrew Marvell*
Chaucer

MISCELLANEOUS

Teaching Poetry: Poetry in Class, Five to Fifteen

Collected Poems of James Reeves 1929–1959

Homage to Trumball Stickney with Séan Haldane

THE
CRITICAL SENSE

PRACTICAL CRITICISM OF
PROSE AND POETRY

by

JAMES REEVES

HEINEMANN
LONDON

Heinemann Educational Books Ltd
LONDON   EDINBURGH   MELBOURNE   TORONTO
SINGAPORE   JOHANNESBURG   HONG KONG
NAIROBI   AUCKLAND   IBADAN
NEW DELHI

ISBN 0 435 18765 1

FIRST PUBLISHED 1956
REPRINTED 1957, 1960, 1961, 1963,
1964, 1966, 1968, 1970

PUBLISHED BY
HEINEMANN EDUCATIONAL BOOKS LTD
48 CHARLES STREET, LONDON WIX 8AH
PRINTED IN GREAT BRITAIN BY
BUTLER AND TANNER LTD., FROME AND LONDON

PREFACE

This is a book of practical criticism for those who wish to increase their appreciation of literature. It is intended both for those studying in a class, and for those reading as individuals with little or no guidance from a teacher. It is to the latter especially that Part I is addressed, since it provides something of the general background of critical theory which members of a class can expect to get from their teacher. It is only against such a background that sound practical work can be done. Readers of Part I are urged to fill in and extend their background knowledge by referring to such fuller critical studies as are mentioned in the bibliography; the subject is a vast and growing one, and can scarcely be more than touched on in a single chapter.

Part II consists of detailed discussion of a number of representative prose passages, supplemented by further examples for critical treatment by the reader. Part III is concerned similarly with poetry. The technical terms which occur in the course of these pages are collected and explained in a glossary.

In writing this book I have had the benefit of much criticism and advice. Some of it has been directly helpful; and all of it has convinced me that no subject is more controversial than literary criticism. Many of the general statements and conclusions have been questioned; and I have fortified myself with the reflection that no single critic, however august and learned, has escaped violent censure at one time or another. I take this as a sign of health; I hope there are many views here expressed which will afford scope for lively discussion.

A more solid basis for satisfaction is that several readers who have expressed disagreement with some of my general conclusions have nevertheless found little to quarrel with in the detailed examination of poems and prose passages. It is here that I hope students—especially those preparing for examinations in practical criticism—will find most help. For it is here that this book differs most from some recent books on the same subject. I might have taken as my starting point the literary critic's armoury of technical terms, and shown how each of them can be handled in attacking any given text. I thought it more fruitful, however, to take a number of texts as my starting point, and see how far we could get without much preliminary weapon-training. To start from the work of art, not the critical principle, is, I claim, to adopt the approach, not of the professional critic, but of the creative writer.

But enough! Rather than risk a controversial engagement at the outset, let us begin this limited reconnaissance into the sacred wood.

J. R.

Chalfont St. Giles
1955

CONTENTS

I

INTRODUCTION

This is a book of applied criticism. In it you are invited to collaborate with the author in criticizing prose and verse. But before we do this we must have some idea what we are about and why we are about it. Why criticize at all? By what means do we apply criticism to literature? Most important of all, how far can we hope to succeed?

Why criticize? Why not simply enjoy books and poems? The answer is: first, because we cannot help criticizing. The fact that we take one book rather than another from the library implies a preference for a particular author or kind of book; and that preference is based on certain critical principles, even if we cannot state exactly what they are. In short, as T. S. Eliot says, 'Criticism is as inevitable as breathing.' Secondly, we shall enjoy literature more if we enjoy it critically. There are many who would dispute this; but on the whole, experience shows that the readers who can at least talk (if not write) intelligently and critically about what they read are the ones who get most out of it. C. Day Lewis is right in insisting that 'appetite must precede discrimination', that you must enjoy something before you begin to think why you enjoy it. Consider the uncritical delight with which a child enjoys a nursery rhyme or a good story. But later, when we are no longer children, our taste is apt to go astray and our enjoyment remain limited, if we do not begin to form at least some general ideas as to why we prefer this writer to that, that poem to this.

Before going further, let us look at two quotations:

2

QUOTATION
1

Since Plato turned his eyes, weary with the flux of things, to a celestial city whose aëry burgomasters kept guard over the perfect and unblemished exemplars of the objects of this bungled world, and not long after, Jesus told his fishermen that they could find their peace only in the Kingdom of Heaven, where the mansions were unnumberable, the subtle and the simple mind alike have been haunted by echoes of an unceasing music and dreams of imperishable beauty. Men's hearts have been swayed between a belief that the echoes and the dreams reached them from a distant eternal world more real than ours, and a premonition that the voice they heard was that of their own soul mysteriously calling them to self-perfection. And even those who have spoken with most conviction and persuasiveness, as though seeing face to face, of the perfect world immune from the rust of time have been the foremost to let fall the warning that their words were a parable. The rare spirits which steer the soul of humanity unite within themselves the contrary impulses of men. They live so intimately with their ideals that they are persuaded of their reality; they think so highly of the soul that a truth for it alone becomes a truth. Therefore they can say in the same breath that the Father's house has many mansions and that the Kingdom of Heaven is within us, and no man can tell for certain whether *The Republic* is an allegory.

This dream or desire is one of the eternal themes of poetry, not because it is superficially more 'poetic' than any other, but because it contains one of the persistent realities of the soul. For if the soul lives in its own right, having a core of active being, it lives by an ideal. There is no escaping the fact of the Kingdom of Heaven which is within you, because it is the condition of the soul's vitality. Once begin to make choice between a worse and a better, and you are inevitably bound to recognize its validity; and to live without making the choice, whatever the intellect may tell us, is not life at all. Life, as we know it, cannot bar the gate against the ideal. If it is a dream it is a dream we live by, and a dream we live by is more real than a reality we ignore.

But if this opposition of the ideal and the real is one of the great essential themes of poetry, it is also one which yields most to the impress of the poet's personality. Between the one pole of a complete belief in the existence of a kingdom of eternal beauty and imperishable perfection, and the other of an unfaltering recognition that these beatitudes exist in and for the soul alone, are infinite possibilities of faith and doubt, inexhaustible opportunities for the creative activity of art. For, apart from the precise mixture of certainty and hesitation in the poet's mind, one of the sovereign gestures of art is to make the ideal real, and to project a dim impersonal awareness on to a structure of definite invention. The sense that we are exiled from our own country, that our rightful heritage has been usurped from us, we know not how, may impel one poet to create his kingdom in words and name it with names, people it with fit inhabitants, and another to record the bare fact of his consciousness as a homeless wanderer.

Mr. de la Mare is a poet of the great theme who is distinguished chiefly by his faculty of pressing invention and fancy to the service of his need. He has named his other kingdom with many names; it is Arabia,

> Where the Princes ride at noon
> 'Mid the verdurous vales and thickets
> Under the ghost of the moon.

It is Tartary; it is Alulvan. Queen Dejanira reigns there, and when she sleeps she walks through

> The courts of the lord Pthamasar,
> Where the sweet birds of Psuthys are.

Or again it is Thule of the old legend, upon which the poet beautifully calls:

> If thou art sweet as they are sad
> > Who on the shore of Time's salt sea
> Watch on the dim horizon fade
> > Ships bearing love and night to thee ...

Within its shifting frontiers are comprised all the dim, debatable lands that lie between the Never-Never country of nursery rhyme and the more solid fields to which the city mind turns for its paradise, the terrestrial happiness which only a shake of the gods' dice-box has denied. ...

JOHN MIDDLETON MURRY

This was written by a sensitive and widely read critic. It is the opening to his appreciation of the poems of Walter de la Mare. It need hardly be said that de la Mare, who died in 1956, was a highly debatable poet and Murry a highly debatable critic—that is, not every intelligent reader agrees as to the value of their work. The point, however, is this. Suppose we are inclined to like de la Mare's poems and wish to know more about them, would Murry's essay on him help us? Yes, something of what the critic says must either illuminate what the poet writes or support or discredit our own impressions. Murry tells us something about de la Mare. He helps us to enjoy him. A critic whom we read later may persuade us that Murry is wrong. Meanwhile, however, our knowledge of de la Mare, of poetry in general, and of literary criticism has been increased, and our power of appreciation strengthened. It does not matter if, in studying Quotation 1, we find the first part difficult. What Murry says is, briefly, that poets are concerned with an ideal world, a world of perfection which lies somewhere outside the world of reality; it is this world which is the subject of de la Mare's poems. One of the poems he mentions is *Arabia*. Let us turn to a second quotation for a different view of this poem. It would be well first to make sure that we have read, and if possible formed an opinion on, the poem in question.

QUOTATION

2

Mr. de la Mare's *Arabia* is even muzzier:

> Far are the shades of Arabia,
>   Where the Princes ride at noon,
> 'Mid the verdurous vales and thickets,
>   Under the ghost of the moon;
>
> And so dark is that vaulted purple
>   Flowers in the forest rise
> And toss into blossom 'gainst the phantom stars
>   Pale in the noonday skies.

If we are to trust travellers, there are no shades in Arabia at noon except during sandstorms. There are no forests. The moon and stars are not visible at noon either there or anywhere else south of the Arctic Circle. The Arabians, Princes and all, do most of their riding at night. Flowers do appear in certain Arabian districts each Spring, but grow low on the ground and are soon burned up.

> Sweet is the music of Arabia
>   In my heart, when out of dreams
> I still in the thin clear murk of dawn
>   Descry her gliding streams;
> Hear her strange lutes on the green banks
>   Ring out loud with the grief and delight
> Of the dim-silked, dark-haired Musicians
>   In the brooding silence of night.

Streams are not characteristic of Arabia except in the short rainy season, when they rush rather than glide. The lute is not an Eastern instrument in spite of the Authorised Version of the

Book of Daniel (where they occur with harps, sackbuts and psalteries); and Arabian music is not sweet, but harsh, bare and monotonous like the desert.

> They haunt me—her lutes and her forests;
>   No beauty on earth I see
> But shadowed with that dream recalls
>   Her loveliness to me:
> Still eyes look coldly upon me,
>   Cold voices whisper and say—
> 'He is crazed with the spell of far Arabia,
>   They have stolen his wits away.'

The perfect modern lyric has a close affinity with the fatigue-dream. If this had been a poem of integrity, the word Arabia would never have been allowed to occur in it; either an actual place would have been chosen, such as Cambodia, where something, though not much, of what he says in the poem applies, or a new name would have been coined. But Mr. de la Mare has had a confused, luxurious dream in which the hackneyed lines 'I'll sing thee songs of Araby and tales of far Cashmere' have developed without any wakeful restraint into this foolish fantasy combining the silken Princes of Araby with the forests, flowers and silks of Cashmere and identifying the 'songs of Araby' with the Victorian song which celebrates them. The last stanza, which admits the craziness of the dream and its distortion of geographical fact, is its best ticket of admission into the popular anthology, where it will continue for many years to *cheat* people of a sigh and *charm* them to a tear.

ROBERT GRAVES

This is part of an account, by a living poet and critic of wide reputation and influence, of certain poems which he regards as having played a considerable part in forming modern poetic taste. It is obvious that he does not think much of *Arabia*, and he gives precise and cogent reasons. Yet Murry regards this same poem as evidence for de la Mare's profound concern with the ideal world which is one of the chief provinces of poetry.

I do not propose to examine these two views of *Arabia*. They are not altogether contradictory, though they would take a good deal of reconciling. The point I want to make is that there is value in studying these two points of view, and in trying to form our own opinion of them. Both quotations should be studied in their context. The intelligent reader may ask, 'If this is literary criticism, what hope have I of forming a reliable judgement?' The answer is, 'It does not so much matter, at this stage, whether your judgement is reliable as that it should be your own.' These two quotations will have helped you if, having known the poem for some years and perhaps enjoyed it uncritically, you forget about it for the time being, but find on returning to it that you like it more, or less, than you used to. This experience with *Arabia* will have helped you in the appreciation of other poems.

3

What is a critic and what is literary criticism? So many answers have been given to these questions that it would be worth while to consider some of them, for upon our view of the function of criticism will depend what value we place on the writings of critics, what we expect to get from reading them, and how much we can expect our own critical efforts to help with the study of literature.

Arnold gives the following definition of the function of criticism:

QUOTATION

3

I am bound by my own definition of criticism: a disinterested endeavour to learn and propagate the best that is known and thought in the world.

Arnold took an authoritarian view of criticism. He regarded the critic as one who should decide what constitutes greatness in literature and should propagate the love of what is good and expose what is second-rate and false. But how is he to decide? By what standards, other than purely personal ones, is he to set up this or that writer as a 'classic'. He himself warned us of the danger of making a purely personal estimate of a work of art, but looking back at his criticism, we see that he was swayed by personal standards much more than he supposed.

Arnold would not have agreed with the remark of the Elizabethan poet Sir Henry Wotton, quoted by Bacon,

QUOTATION

4

That critics are like brushers of noblemen's clothes.

In other words, they are concerned with tidying up and embellishing something they did not make themselves and does not belong to them. Arnold had a high view of the function of criticism, but this view was not held by many before him. For a long time criticism was regarded as a parasitic activity. Dryden, whom Dr. Johnson called the father of English criticism, wrote:

QUOTATION

5

Ill Writers are usually the sharpest Censors; For they (as the best Poet, and the best Patron said), When in the full perfection of decay, turn Vinegar, and come again in Play. Thus the corruption of a Poet is the Generation of a Critick: I mean of a Critick in the general acceptation of this Age; for formerly they were quite another Species of Men. They were Defenders of Poets, and Commentators on their Works: to Illustrate obscure

Beauties; to place some passages in a better light; to redeem others from malicious Interpretations: to help out an Author's Modesty, who is not ostentatious of his Wit; and, in short, to shield him from the Ill-Nature of those Fellows, who ... now take upon themselves the Venerable name of Censors.

JOHN DRYDEN, 1693

Byron expressed scorn for the professional critic in his poem *English Bards and Scotch Reviewers*:

QUOTATION
6

A man must serve his time to every trade
Save censure—critics all are ready made.

The poets of Byron's time suffered severely from the censure of unsympathetic critics, and there is considerable point in Byron's sarcasm. These lines should serve as a warning against all uninformed censure of modern art. If you go to any exhibition of modern painting, you will hear much hostile comment from people who clearly do not want to understand what they are looking at. The Scotch critics whom Byron attacked really hated the whole Romantic school of poetry which Byron represented. They did harm by parading their personal dislikes under the guise of critical judgements. Coleridge echoes Byron's hostility to such critics, and repeats Dryden's suggestion that critics are creative artists who have failed.

QUOTATION
7

Reviewers are usually people who would have been poets, historians, biographers, &c., if they could; they have tried their talents at one or the other, and have failed; therefore they turn critics.

The same point was made forcibly by Benjamin Disraeli:

QUOTATION
8

You know who the critics are? The men who have failed in literature and art.

There has always existed a certain rivalry, if not hostility, between critics and other writers. Yet creative writing and criticism are not fundamentally opposed. Dryden saw that criticism had a true function as the handmaid of creative writing. It was only when critics set themselves up as independent authorities that they incurred the hatred of writers. The best critics are indeed also creative writers. Arnold expressed his sense of the high importance of criticism, but he was himself a poet who tried to put into practice the critical canons he laid down. It is since Arnold's time that the notion of the critic not as judge but as interpreter has been generally accepted. This view is expressed by the French writer Anatole France:

QUOTATION
9

The good critic is he who relates the adventures of his soul among masterpieces.

This view is worth studying. It appears to be the view held by Murry (see Quotation 1), for the attitude Murry adopts is that of one who has been deeply moved by what he has read and seeks to express his sense of its worth and communicate it to others. This view implies that the critic cannot remain detached from what he interprets. Most of Murry's best criticism is highly personal and enthusiastic. He seems to say: 'This work has moved me deeply. Here is what I have felt about it. I have little use for detached and scientific analysis. If you regard me as a sensitive and widely experienced reader, you will appreciate what I say, and your enjoyment of what I praise will be made richer and fuller.' Murry does not seek to reason with those who have no use for his judgements. He has loved certain books and writers and wants you to share his love.

But the method of love has its dangers. It is possible to be uncritically enthusiastic about something quite worthless. James Russell Lowell wrote:

QUOTATION
10

A wise scepticism is the first attribute of a good critic.

That is, a good critic is cautious. Murry has little use for caution. If anything, he is over-enthusiastic. Is this what is called a good fault? Yes, provided we have read a good deal ourselves and know where to discount enthusiasm. The important word in the quotation from Anatole France is adventures'. To critics of Murry's kind the sense of adventure in reading is uppermost. If life is not an adventure, and consequently literature also, it is of little importance; adventure implies curiosity and exploration. If we are not prepared to explore in literature, we miss most of what it offers.

Yet the search for real standards, independent of personal enthusiasm and preference, continues, and in practice we all try to form such standards. In merely giving a reason why we like such and such a poem we imply that there are objective reasons for doing so. If we say a description is good because it is vivid, we assume that vividness is a test of good description. Whether or not we can or should ever try to discount personal feelings and tastes, we must, in practice, think and talk as if we could do so. Otherwise criticism is no more than saying, 'I like this because I like it.'

The tendency in modern criticism has been to try to analyse the writer's intentions and motives, conscious or unconscious, and to leave the result to the judgement of intelligent readers. Modern critics of the school of I. A. Richards are in the main content to analyse as exactly and fully as possible what the writer says, insisting that perfect understanding must precede judgement. In *The Art of Fiction* Henry James writes:

QUOTATION

11

> We must grant the artist his subject, his idea, his *donné*: our criticism is applied only to what he makes of it.

This statement is the summary of an important view of criticism. It implies that what matters is not *what* the writer says but *how* he says it. What James says about fiction is echoed by the modern poet A. E. Housman in his lecture *The Name and Nature of Poetry*.

QUOTATION

12

> Poetry is not the thing said, but a way of saying it.

This view suggests that a critic should confine himself to technical considerations and leave the question of subject matter alone. The themes of art, according to this view, are limited in number and repeated throughout the centuries. One poet differs from another not in the subject of his poetry but in his treatment. It is, indeed, the difference of their approach to a single theme that constitutes the difference between writers of different periods. The journey of Ulysses from Troy back to his home in Ithaca, and all the adventures that befell him, are the subject of Homer's *Odyssey*, which may be taken as Homer's view of the progress of a man's soul. A day in the life of two men in Dublin early in the present century is the subject of James Joyce's *Ulysses* which, as the choice of title implies, is also the story of man's adventuring soul. The difference between the two writers' versions of the same story may be taken as a measure of the difference in temperament between the early Greeks and modern Western man.

4

We must, as Day Lewis has said, enjoy before we can criticize; but we must, by the time we begin to grow up, develop our critical sense along with our sense of enjoyment. The two will grow together and nourish one another. We should regard the critic not as a divinely inspired authority nor as a mere parasite; we should look upon him as a reader like ourselves who has read and thought widely and asked himself the reasons for his enthusiasm for the writers he praises. His function is not to arbitrate, to dictate, but to explain and illuminate. The good critic is not one who casts aside all personal predilection, even though he may try to think and write as if he could do so; he admits with humility that he may never achieve finality, even though he must write as if he could do so; he must admit that his is not the only view, even though it may be the only one that makes sense to him; he must recognize that owing to the limitations of his personality he cannot see all there is to be seen in a complex work of art, and many of the best and most interesting works of art, especially of literary art, are highly complex. All he can hope to do, and all we can expect of him, is that he will show us something in a work of art that we had not seen before; or make us like an author we had previously neglected;

or add one more point of view to the many already expressed on his subject.

This many-sidedness of art and of criticism, however, and the practical impossibility of reaching final conclusions and formulating simple tests of value, does not mean that our attitude to art and criticism should be weak, vacillating and sloppy. That we cannot formulate exact standards does not mean that we must not try to find them; that no one can say the last word on *Hamlet* does not mean that no one should think about it at all; that two critics disagree, however, does not necessarily mean that they are equally good critics. One will be more illuminating than the other. As readers, we must try to judge between them. In all we read we should cultivate the critical sense, remembering that criticism does not mean censure. To explain a difficult poem, to show the reasons why something has moved him, to analyse the construction of a good novel or play, and in Dryden's phrase 'to illustrate obscure beauties'—these tasks are as much the function of the critic as to point out faults and condemn weaknesses—indeed, I would say, more so. A good critic is chary of mere condemnation. This is right and necessary if the critic can show what is good only by first pointing out what is bad. There are times when severe censure is a duty of the critic. Lord Macaulay enjoyed himself wholeheartedly at the expense of the poet Montgomery when he saw that Montgomery's sort of poetry was corrupting the taste for what was good. Robert Graves attacked what he thought was bad in the Georgian poetry anthologies when he felt that they were destroying the taste for true poetry; and much of the destructive criticism of the 1920's and 1930's has had a salutary effect, making possible the appreciation of such poets as Gerard Manley Hopkins and E. E. Cummings.

We should not be afraid of cultivating the critical sense.

We often hear the warning that criticism destroys enjoyment. Some who like bad poetry would prefer to be left unenlightened. So too would lovers of good poetry. I have often heard it said that to analyse a sonnet by Shakespeare or an ode of Keats destroys it. But I have never met anyone whose real enjoyment of a good poem has been spoilt by criticism. Those who object to the criticism of art may be lazy-minded, or they may be afraid of losing something which they do not wholly possess. For the love of any work of art is not really secure if it will not stand up to questioning. If a person tells you that he considers worthless a book or a poem which you like, do not refuse to hear him. Let him tell you why he thinks nothing of it; then ask him what he *does* admire, and why. For if a critic attacks merely for the sake of destruction, you can be sure that there is something wrong with his standards; if on the other hand he can show you that what you like is bad and that to like it may be hindering you from appreciating something better, then he is worth listening to. In the end, the only thing that can destroy a taste for the bad is the appreciation of the good. Constructive criticism is more valuable than destructive.

So do not think of the critical sense as something destructive, something that is going to crush the bloom of your enjoyment. The bloom on an aesthetic sensation is not so easily destroyed as that on a peach or a butterfly. The critical sense is not a carping, hair-splitting faculty; it is the faculty of seeing, at least in part, *why* we enjoy something a great deal, and something else more, and something else less. It is an insight, partly instinctive and partly trained, into the mind and art of the writer, which shows us what he is trying to do and how he does it. It gives us pleasure in the ways in which words are put together. It cannot create enjoyment; no critic can *make* you like something that is temperamentally abhorrent to you. No critic has ever made me like Byron or Scott, and it would be as insincere in me to pretend I thought as much of them as did their first enthusiasts, as to pretend there are not readers as intelligent as I who enjoy them immensely. But criticism can help us to realize why we like something, and this increases our liking; it can give us a sense of community with sensitive minds by showing that we are not alone in our liking; it can encourage us to try authors whom we have hitherto avoided; it can enrich and stimulate that continuous intercourse between our own personality and that of others, as expressed in literature, which gives to our reading the sense of discovery and excitement without which it is the mere passing of time. Literature helps us to understand life, and criticism helps us to understand literature.

A concluding word on the danger of too much criticism: read criticism either to illuminate literature already read, or to introduce literature not yet read. Do not read criticism for ready-made judgements or as a substitute for literature. Develop your own critical sense; do not rely on that of others. The main purpose of this book is to encourage the development of your own judgement and the formation of your own standards. It is not a guide to the literary criticism of others. Its object is to suggest some ideas about the art of writing, and some ways in which the reader can apply them to what he reads. It is the poet, the novelist, the dramatist who creates enjoyment, not the critic. The critic's function is to assist the reader in an active participation in the writer's work. Only by developing his own critical sense can the reader be sure of the fullest pleasure from such a participation.

FOR DISCUSSION

1. Of what value is uncritical appreciation?

2. Should parents and teachers allow children to read what they like? Consider Day Lewis's statement that 'Appetite must precede discrimination' in the light of what you know about American comics; and consider Dr. Johnson's remarks:

> 'I am always for getting a boy forward in his learning; for that is a sure good. I would let him at first read *any* English book which happens to engage his attention; because you have done a great deal when you have brought him to entertainment from a book. He'll get better books afterwards.'
>
> (1779)

3. Discuss the account of de la Mare's *Arabia* contained in Quotation 2 (p. 5).

4. Consider Quotation 6 (p. 9). What training would you suggest for the work of literary criticism?

5. Consider Bacon's advice: 'Read not to contradict and confute; nor to believe and take for granted; nor to find talk and discourse; but to weigh and consider.' (Essay *Of Studies*, 1597.)

6. Consider Quotations 11 and 12 (p. 12), and then compare the following poems:

(a)

To the Virgins, to make much of Time

Gather ye Rose-buds, while ye may,
    Old Time is still a-flying:
And this same flower that smiles to-day
    To-morrow will be dying.

The glorious Lamp of Heaven, the Sun,
    The higher he's a getting;
The sooner will his Race be run,
    And nearer he's to Setting.

That Age is best which is the first,
　　When Youth and Blood are warmer;
But being spent, the worse, and worst
　　Times, still succeed the former.

Then be not coy, but use your time;
　　And while ye may, goe marry:
For having lost but once your prime,
　　You may for ever tarry.

Robert Herrick

(b)

Blue Girls

Twirling your blue skirts, travelling the sward
Under the towers of your seminary,
Go listen to your teachers old and contrary
Without believing a word.

Tie the white fillets then about your hair
And think no more of what will come to pass
Than bluebirds that go walking on the grass
And chattering on the air.

Practise your beauty, blue girls, before it fail,
And I will cry with my loud lips and publish
Beauty which all our power shall never establish,
It is so frail.

For I could tell you a story which is true
I know a lady with a terrible tongue,
Blear eyes fallen from blue,
All her perfections tarnished—yet it is not long
Since she was lovelier than any of you.

John Crowe Ransom

II

THE CRITICISM OF PROSE

I

It may be helpful (provided we do not push the comparison too far) to think of literature as an enormous and still growing mansion. The different rooms are occupied by the works of different writers. An alert person, the moment he enters a new room, is aware of its atmosphere, its style. As we enter into a new book and savour its style, we ask ourselves, Is this a style I like? Could I get on with this style, or shall I find it repellent? A room always gives a clue to the character, tastes, and temperament of the owner. Here is a comfortable, untidy room full of interesting things in every sort of disorder; the owner, we feel, is an easy-going, entertaining person—we could get on all right with him or her, though perhaps he would be too disorderly and undependable in his habits to make a life-long friend. Here is a pleasant room—airy, light, furnished with originality and without affectation; its owner must be the sort of person I would like to know. A third room is stuffy, over-formal; we should never be comfortable here; the owner is obviously a stickler for etiquette and probably likes only the company of scholars. A fourth room is fussy, over-furnished—rather amusing for a short time, but we could never settle down in it. Here is a dull room, conventionally furnished, the pictures on the walls just like everyone else's. The next room belongs to a person of highly original tastes, yet obviously a restless person; his room gives no sense of repose; nothing is comfortable, everything odd, ill-fitting, ill-assorted. The curtains clash with the carpet, the pictures swear at the walls. We may like the owner violently at first sight, then quarrel with equal violence, and part from him for ever.

As with the style of a room, so with the style of a writer. Some we like instinctively but soon tire of; some we dislike at first, then grow to enjoy; some writers become lifelong friends, and their style remains a room we are never tired of visiting and re-visiting.

It would take too long to discuss all the functions of prose, the aims of every important writer, and the means by which he tries to achieve his aims. The best that can be done briefly is to examine a number of prose passages from a variety of books, in order that we may form some general principles which can be applied to the prose of other writers and periods. We shall attempt to develop and sharpen the critical sense by examining critically a variety of passages. We shall see how our general liking or disliking of an author can be expressed in critical terms.

It must be stressed, however, that we can in a limited space assess only the especial quality of a given writer's style: we cannot judge of complete prose works, such as a novel, an essay, or a short story. That is something beyond the scope of this book.

When we come to discuss poems (see Part III), we shall be dealing with complete works, brief though they may be. It will thus be possible to judge of what the poet is saying, as well as of how he says it. In discussing short prose extracts, however, the emphasis will necessarily be on form, rather than on content; on the means of expression, rather than on what is being expressed. Here we approach one of the central paradoxes of literary criticism: in any work of art, form and content are inseparable, yet the critic must separate them. He will speak now of content—what the book or poem is about; now of form—how the writer expresses the content.

He cannot speak of the two together, any more than we can see both sides of a coin simultaneously. In a poem or a piece of prose we cannot alter form without altering content, however slightly. This has been noticed by critics again and again: it is what they mean when they say that matter and style are one. If, therefore, in criticizing a prose passage we discuss its style, it must be remembered that we are really thinking also of its content. This will not be obvious in the early stages of our discussion of prose, but it will be increasingly evident as the examples we take become more subtle, more complex and more personal.

2

The following is a paragraph from Sir John Gielgud's essay on the production of Wilde's *The Importance of Being Earnest*. Gielgud, as a professional actor and producer, is concerned solely with making his point as clearly and concisely as possible. He is discussing the important matter of *pace* in the production of a comedy of manners.

QUOTATION
13

The pace of the comedy must be leisurely, mannered; and everybody must, of course, speak beautifully—but the wit must appear spontaneous, though self-conscious. The text must be studied and spoken so as to arouse a cumulative effect of laughter from the audience. That is to say it may be sometimes necessary to sacrifice laughs on certain witty lines in order that a big laugh may come at the end of a passage, rather than to extract two or three small ones in between, which may dissipate the sense and retard the progress of the dialogue. There are, if anything, too many funny lines, and the actor may easily ruin a passage by allowing the audience to laugh in the middle. For instance, the following sally in the first act:

JACK: My dear Algy, you talk exactly as if you were a dentist.

> It is very vulgar to talk like a dentist when one isn't a
> dentist. It produces a false impression.
> ALGERNON: Well, that is exactly what dentists always do.

If the actors leave time for the audience to laugh after the words
'It produces a false impression', Algernon's reply will fall flat
and seem redundant. Actors with expert pace and timing will
hurry the dialogue, Algernon breaking in quickly with his line,
so that the audience may not laugh until he has spoken it.

This is practical advice, given in a practical manner, without stylistic flourishes. Gielgud describes the type of speech
which the actors should employ, makes his main point about
getting laughs, and concludes with a quotation from the text
to illustrate this point.

Prose is here used, not for artistic effect, not for the expression of personality, but for communicating information. In
short it is prose doing its ordinary, everyday job.

Here is a further example of prose used in the same way.
It is from the article on *The Moon* written by one of the
anonymous contributors to *The Oxford Junior Encyclopædia*.
The interest of the passage comes from the subject-matter,
not the writing; this is as it should be, for the author is concerned solely with accurate scientific exposition. Yet he could
not achieve this without a sound working knowledge of the
English language.

QUOTATION

14

Through the earliest telescopes the surface of the Moon was
seen to consist of mountains and darker areas, apparently seas.
These were fancifully called by such names as Mare Imbrium
and Mare Nubium. Later and better telescopes showed that the
'seas' were not perfectly level and must really be plains. In the

lunar southern hemisphere the rings and craters lie overlapping in great confusion. The northern hemisphere shows some splendid mountain-ranges and immense plains walled in by jagged heights. The highest peak in the Moon, Newton, is 24,000 feet high. Such heights can be measured by the lengths of the shadows cast. No one knows for certain how the walled plains and craters and bright rays have been formed. The craters are not very like those of volcanoes on the Earth—but the force of gravity is so much less on the Moon that we should hardly expect them to be. Some people suppose that a great shower of projectiles, perhaps meteorites, struck and damaged the Moon, leaving scars which do indeed look something like bomb craters, and which also resemble the few meteorite craters found on the Earth. Others think that the craters may have been formed by bubbles of gas rising from the interior of the Moon and bursting on the surface in ages past when this was still only semi-solid.

3

Straightforward writing of this sort we judge by the ease and speed with which we can read and understand it. If it is clumsy or obscure, either the writer does not know his job or else he is writing hastily. The difficulty of writing such prose depends partly but not wholly on the complexity of the subject-matter. It is not always easy to explain a simple matter clearly. On the whole, the success with which a writer composes everyday prose depends on the skill, patience and experience with which he handles the language.

The sort of prose we have discussed so far has been called 'straightforward' and 'everyday'. It is utilitarian prose; we do not look to it for style and personality. Its style, if it has style, consists in the absence of literary devices; the personality of the writer is best expressed when it does not obtrude itself.

Much prose, however, is not of this utilitarian kind. It may strive for literary effect; it may aim at moving as well as informing the reader; it may be a vehicle for the writer's personality. Indeed, most writers would find it hard to keep their personality out of their writing, even if they so wished. Many write as if they were aiming at the objective presentation of the truth; but most see the truth through the medium of their own personality. They cannot help doing so; and this medium may distort or colour the truth with prejudice, incomplete knowledge, conscious or unconscious dishonesty, or the desire to persuade. This is particularly liable to happen in writing of a political character.

QUOTATION

15

I lay it down as a maxim, that for a family to be happy, they must be well supplied with food and raiment. It is a sorry effort that people make to persuade others or to persuade themselves, that they can be happy in a state of want of the necessaries of life. The doctrines which fanaticism preaches, and which teach men to be content with poverty, have a very pernicious tendency, and are calculated to favour tyrants by giving them passive slaves. To live well, to enjoy all things that make life pleasant, is the right of every man who constantly uses his strength judiciously and lawfully. It is to blaspheme God to suppose that he created men to be miserable, to hunger, thirst, and perish with cold, in the midst of that abundance which is the fruit of their own labour. Instead, therefore, of applauding 'happy poverty', which applause is so much the fashion of the present day, I despise the man that is poor and contented; for such is a certain proof of a base disposition, a disposition which is the enemy of all industry, all exertion, all love of independence.

WILLIAM COBBETT

This is an example of downright, hard-hitting argument, intended not so much to persuade by sweet reasonableness as to hammer home a point. It is rhetorical tub-thumping; its keynote is a manly scorn. The language is strong and vigorous; there are very few adjectives—only one or two are used descriptively (e.g. 'a *base* disposition'), the others for the most part being used predicatively (e.g. 'the man that is *poor* and *contented*').

The length of the sentences suggests that the author is thinking and writing at some speed: they contain, respectively, 23, 30, 30, 25, 35, and 52 words. The author is not one to compress his thought into a short sentence; on the contrary, his style is ample and repetitive. The following is an analysis of the argument:

1st sentence: statement that material sufficiency is necessary to happiness.

2nd: re-statement in more downright terms.

3rd: attack on low church social doctrines, and warning against political tyranny.

4th: repetition of original statement with qualifying clause, 'who constantly uses his strength', etc.

5th: appeal to religion.

6th: attempt to sum up previous points. The word 'therefore' gives an appearance of logical thought, but in reality the argument is not strictly logical: the idea that to be poor and contented shows a base disposition does not follow from the previous statements, but is a fresh idea thrown in for good measure to ram the argument home.

This is part of the introduction to *Cottage Economy*, an excellent book of practical advice written by William Cobbett and published in 1821 for the benefit of the cottage farmers who had suffered so badly from the results of war and enclosure, and whose plight he felt so passionately. Logical argument was not his strong point. He attempts to convert rather by the vigour of his indignation in whatever cause he is advocating, and by the force of his own conviction. He was a political journalist, and in his last years an M.P., and he dealt in plain-spoken rhetoric rather than subtle dialectic.

4

Let us look at a passage by a contemporary of Cobbett. It is, on the whole, utilitarian writing; its aim is to inform. But it is a personal narrative, and through the more or less objective quality of the writing appears something of the writer's personality.

QUOTATION
16

... I set off for the village; where I found to my great mortification, that no person would admit me into his house. I was regarded with astonishment and fear, and was obliged to sit all day without victuals, in the shade of a tree; and the night threatened to be very uncomfortable, for the wind rose, and there was great appearance of heavy rain; and the wild beasts are so very numerous in the neighbourhood, that I should have been under the necessity of climbing up the tree, and resting among the branches. About sunset, however, as I was preparing to pass the night in this manner, and had turned my horse loose, that he might graze at liberty, a woman, returning from the labours of the field, stopped to observe me, and perceiving that I was weary and dejected, inquired into my situation, which I briefly explained to her; whereupon, with looks of great compassion, she took up my saddle and bridle, and told me to follow her. Having conducted me into her hut, she lighted up a lamp, spread a mat on the floor, and told me I might remain there for the night. Finding that I was very hungry, she said she would procure me something to eat. She accordingly went out and returned in a short time with a very fine fish; which having caused to be half-broiled upon some embers, she gave me for supper. The rites of hospitality being thus performed towards a stranger in distress, my worthy benefactress (pointing to the mat, and telling me I might sleep there without apprehension) called to the female part of her family, who had stood gazing on me all the while in fixed astonishment, to resume their task of spinning cotton; in which they continued to employ themselves great part of the night. They lightened their labour by songs, one of which was composed extempore; for I was myself the subject of it. It was sung by one of the young women, the rest joining in a sort of chorus. The air was sweet and plaintive, and the words, literally translated, were these:— 'The winds roared, and the rains fell. The poor white man, faint and weary, came and sat under our tree. He has no mother to bring him milk; no wife to grind his corn.' *Chorus*—'Let us pity the white man; no mother has he,' etc. etc. Trifling as this recital may appear to the reader, to a person in my situation, the circumstance was affecting in the highest degree. I was oppressed by such unexpected kindness; and sleep fled from my eyes. In the morning I presented my compassionate land-lady with two of the four brass buttons which remained on my waistcoat; the only recompense I could make her.

Mungo Park, 1799

Mungo Park, born in 1771 and killed by negroes in 1806, was one of the first British explorers in Africa. In 1799 he published an account of his journey to the Niger. He was not a professional writer, like his friend Sir Walter Scott, but a naval doctor of good education who had been to Edinburgh University. He wrote, not for artistic effect, but to tell a plain tale of remarkable adventures.

His style is the standard prose of a late eighteenth-century gentleman with no literary pretensions. Clarity and exactness were its aims, to be achieved while observing literary propriety: this meant using the language and sentence-constructions which Dr. Johnson would have used. To us the sentences seem long and complex, the language in places

stilted and latinized. The following is an analysis of the
number of clauses in each sentence (that is, in each group of
words terminated by a full stop).

1st sentence: 3 clauses	8th sentence: 3 clauses
2nd: 7	9th: 1
3rd: 8	10th: 3 (counting the song
4th: 3	as only one clause)
5th: 2	11th: 2
6th: 3	12th: 2
7th: 4	13th: 3

Notice that, apart from the words of the song, only one
sentence consists of a single clause. The rest contain from
two to eight. Many of the clauses are amplified by the use of
participial phrases, such as 'perceiving that I was weary and
dejected', 'having conducted me into her hut', and 'finding
that I was very hungry'. The simple structure of the native
song is in marked contrast to the complicated European
structure of Park's own writing.

The long third sentence contains the following words of
Romance (Latin or French) origin: labour, observe, perceive,
dejected, inquired, situation, explain, compassion. True, it
contains also the following words of Germanic origin: turn,
horse, loose, graze, woman, field, stopped, weary, looks,
saddle, bridle, told, follow. But the proportion of 'Latin'
words is higher than would nowadays be considered normal
in writing of a simple, narrative kind. The periphrasis in 'my
worthy benefactress' and 'my compassionate landlady' is also
a mark of its time.

In spite of all this, however, Park's style was direct, and
what is sometimes called 'masculine', free from affectation
and obscurity. His story proceeds naturally and easily, without digressions and without excessive bareness; he is never

pompous and never dull; he never betrays an attitude of superiority or condescension towards the natives; and if he is sometimes pious, his piety is sincere. He is modest, but without false modesty. He writes frankly, but without exaggeration, of his own hardships and sufferings. He frequently refers to his own feelings, but rather in set phrases than with minute psychological insight. 'To my great mortification', 'I was weary and dejected', 'the circumstance was affecting in the highest degree', 'oppressed by such unexpected kindness'—in such expressions he refers to his feelings, leaving the reader to imagine the details. After all, he is exploring Africa, not the human mind.

We may say, then, that the style is that of an educated gentleman of his time using prose purely as a medium for communicating a narrative of fact and discovery to an educated audience. If a modern writer used this style, we should think him affected. The journalistic traveller of to-day, describing the same incident, would be more likely to express himself somewhat as follows:

> When I got to the village, I found no one would take me in. They were evidently afraid of me. I had to sit under a tree all day with no food. There were wild animals about, so it looked as if I should have to pass the night in the branches. I did not relish this, for it looked like being a stormy night. I turned my horse loose to graze. At sunset a native woman came back from the fields. She asked me what my trouble was. I told her and she looked sorry. Picking up my saddle and bridle, she told me to follow her. When we got to her hut, she lit a lamp, and gave me a mat to sleep on. Then she went out and brought back a fine fish, cooked it on the remains of a fire, and gave it me to eat.

And so on. Whether we prefer Mungo Park or the modern traveller is a matter of taste.

5

As an example of much more complex thought and more literary writing, let us look at the following.

QUOTATION
17

The youth stared at the land in front of him. Its foliages now seemed to veil powers and horrors. He was unaware of the machinery of orders that started the charge, although from the corners of his eyes he saw an officer, who looked like a boy a-horseback, come galloping, waving his hat. Suddenly he felt a straining and heaving among the men. The line fell slowly forward like a toppling wall, and, with a convulsive gasp that was intended for a cheer, the regiment began its journey.

The youth was pushed and jostled for a moment before he understood the movement at all, but directly he lunged ahead and began to run.

He fixed his eye upon a distant prominent clump of trees where he had concluded the enemy were to be met, and he ran toward it as toward a goal. He had believed throughout that it was a mere question of getting over an unpleasant matter as quickly as possible, and he ran desperately, as if pursued for a murder. His face was drawn hard and tight with the stress of his endeavour. His eyes were fixed in a lurid glare. And with his soiled and disordered dress, his red and inflamed features surmounted by the dingy rag with its spot of blood, his wildly-swinging rifle and banging accoutrements, he looked to be an insane soldier.

As the regiment swung from its position out into a cleared space, the woods and thickets before it awakened. Yellow flames leaped toward it from many directions. The forest made a tremendous objection.

The line lurched straight for a moment. Then the right wing swung forward; it in turn was surpassed by the left. Afterward the centre careered to the front until the regiment was a wedge-shaped mass, but an instant later the opposition of the bushes, trees and uneven places on the ground split the command and scattered it into detached clusters.

The youth, light-footed, was unconsciously in advance. His eyes still kept note of the clump of trees. From all places near it the clannish yell of the enemy could be heard. The little flames of rifles leaped from it. The song of the bullets was in the air, and shells snarled among the treetops. One tumbled directly into the middle of a hurrying group and exploded in crimson fury. There was an instant's spectacle of a man, almost over it, throwing up his hands to shield his eyes.

STEPHEN CRANE

In his novel, *The Red Badge of Courage*, Stephen Crane, a young American writer of the late nineteenth century, described some of the fighting in the American Civil War. He was too young to have seen anything of the Civil War, and his account is based on eye-witness reports and written records. It is an imaginative reconstruction, and the action is seen and felt in the person of 'the youth' who is the hero of the story. Two world wars have taken place since Crane died, and we are used to realistic accounts of fighting. But in Crane's day a romantic aura still clung round the idea of soldiering. His novel was the first to show the soldier as an ordinary man, cowardly by nature, courageous when necessary, helpless in war's ruthless and inhuman grip. (Bernard Shaw's anti-romantic comedy, *Arms and the Man*, appeared shortly after it.)

Crane's style is calm and objective. Yet the horror and destruction of war are all the more clearly expressed because of this dispassionate style of writing. The writer is not himself cold or detached; he writes rather as if he were holding back his feelings and letting events make their own impression.

Crane achieves his purpose by a skilful mixture of the concrete and the abstract. Consider on the one hand the vivid
snapshots contained in the references to the officer waving his
hat, the distant clump of trees, the eyes of the youth 'fixed
in a lurid glare', his dingy bandage with its spot of blood,
the yellow flames, the man shielding his eyes from the explod-
ing shell; and on the other hand, consider the more abstract
suggestion in 'Its foliages now seemed to veil powers and
horrors' and 'He had believed throughout that it was a mere
question of getting over an unpleasant matter as quickly as
possible'. Consider also in its context the statement 'The
forest made a tremendous objection'. In terms of physical
fact this means that the advancing men met with heavy gun-
fire from enemy positions in the forest. Expressed in the more
abstract way, however, it implies that the forest itself resisted
their advance in a terrifying way; it reinforces the previous
observation, 'Its foliages now seemed to veil powers and
horrors.'

This kind of writing may deceive us into thinking that it is
simpler than it is. But notice how its effect is carefully
heightened by simile and comparison: 'The line fell slowly
forward like a toppling wall' and 'he ran desperately, as if
pursued for a murder'. In the first example there is a suggestion that the regiment's advance begins involuntarily, impelled
by some outer force; in the second there is the suggestion
that the youth is obsessed by fear and guilt. Notice also the
skilful use of short sentences among longer ones, which conveys something of the irregularity, hesitations, and nervous
tension of the action.

This kind of writing may be summed up as a narrative of
action, with an undercurrent of psychological comment; this
is effected by a combination of vivid, carefully selected
physical detail with occasional abstract suggestion.

6

In the next quotation we move much further in the direction of a highly subjective and personal style.

QUOTATION
18

The car ploughed uphill through the long squalid straggle of Tevershall, the blackened brick dwellings, black slate roofs glistening their sharp edges, the mud black with coal-dust, the pavements wet and black. It was as if dismalness had soaked through and through everything. The utter negation of natural beauty, the utter negation of the gladness of life, the utter absence of the instinct for shapely beauty which every bird and beast has, the utter death of the human intuitive faculty was appalling. The stacks of soap in the grocers' shops, the rhubarb and lemons in the greengrocers! the awful hats in the milliners! all went by ugly, ugly, ugly, followed by the plaster and gilt horror of the cinema with its wet picture announcements, *A Woman's Love*, and the new big Primitive chapel, primitive enough in its stark brick and big panes of greenish and raspberry glass in the windows. The Wesleyan chapel, higher up, was of blackened brick and stood behind iron railings and blackened shrubs. The Congregational chapel, which thought itself superior, was built of rusticated sandstone and had a steeple, not a very high one. Just beyond were the new school buildings, expensive pink brick, and gravelled playground inside iron railings, all very imposing, and mixing the suggestion of a chapel and a prison.

D. H. LAWRENCE

This is a description of a mining village in the Midlands, of the kind which sprang up in the nineteenth century when the coalfields were being exploited without regard for design or beauty. Lawrence is here concerned to give a picture or soul-destroying squalor and ugliness. He chooses a rainy day, which adds to the effect of depression, but such days are common in the Midlands. He makes no attempt to be detached and objective, but stamps upon every sentence his own loathing and disgust. The objects in the description and the words used to project them on to the reader's eye are deliberately selected to heighten this impression. There is nothing for which he can find a good word. Not only does he describe the physical horror of Tevershall, he comments also on the social snobbery which exists between rival chapel congregations and the cultural philistinism which builds a new school in the likeness of a combined chapel and prison.

There is, moreover, the expression of a feeling of despair and hopelessness about life in a community of this sort, with its 'utter negation of natural beauty, the utter negation of the gladness of life, the utter absence of the instinct for shapely beauty which every bird and beast has, the utter death of the human intuitive faculty'. There is savage irony in the choice of a film title, *A Woman's Love*—as if anything could exist there which ought to be natural, warm, and human.

Lawrence's aim is to make the reader share directly in his own sensation; to this end he makes his style as forceful as possible, mainly by the use of words suggestive of his feelings ('squalid', 'horror', 'appalling'); by selecting for notice such things as the two sourest fruits, rhubarb and lemon, and ugly manifestations of commercial art, such as 'greenish and raspberry' chapel windows, and the 'plaster and gilt' cinema; and by repetition—'utter' occurs four times, 'ugly', 'black' and 'blackened' three times each. The metaphor in 'the car *ploughed* uphill' suggests a difficult progress through thick, clogging mud.

7

He looked northward towards Howth. The sea had fallen below the line of seawrack on the shallow side of the breakwater and already the tide was running out fast along the foreshore. Already one long oval bank of sand lay warm and dry amid the wavelets. Here and there warm isles of sand gleamed above the shallow tides and about the isles and around the long bank and amid the shallow currents of the bridge were lightclad figures, wading and delving.

In a few moments he was barefoot, his stockings folded in his pockets, and his canvas shoes dangling by their knotted laces over his shoulders and, picking a pointed salteaten stick out of the jetsam among the rocks, he clambered down the slope of the breakwater.

There was a long rivulet in the strand and, as he waded slowly up its course, he wondered at the endless drift of seaweed. Emerald and black and russet and olive, it moved beneath the current, swaying and turning. The water of the rivulet was dark with endless drift and mirrored the highdrifting clouds. The clouds were drifting above him silently and silently the seatangle was drifting below him; and the grey warm air was still: and a new wild life was singing in his veins.

JAMES JOYCE

It appears from the last clause in this passage that the man referred to is at some point of crisis or excitement in his life. The seashore scene which is the background for this mental experience is perceived and described with extraordinary clarity. The reader is made vividly aware of the open, airy seascape—the islands of sand appearing above the retreating tide, the multi-coloured seaweed, the water, the clouds, and the beachcombers. Very little feeling is conveyed directly by the choice of words: compare, for instance, Lawrence's description of Tevershall (Quotation 18); the writing is objective. Yet there is a subtle emotional undercurrent, and out of the language of the description, and more especially perhaps its rhythm, emerges something of the exhilaration of mind which bursts forth in the last ten words. There is something in the following sequence of words which prepares us, however slightly, for the climax—'warm and dry', 'wavelets', 'gleamed', 'mirrored', 'highdrifting', 'grey warm air'. It would at least have been a surprise to the reader if instead of 'a new wild life was singing in his veins', the last words had been 'a feeling of dejection came over him'.

The writing is vivid, but not photographically precise. It is impressionistic. The proportion of finite verbs and concrete nouns to adjectives and participles is low. In the nine sentences which this passage contains only one has four clauses, one has three, and the rest two or one each. The greater part of the sense of the passage is conveyed in long adjectival and adverbial phrases: 'below the line of seawrack', 'on the shallow side of the breakwater', 'along the foreshore', 'warm and dry amid the wavelets', 'above the shallow tides', 'about the isles and around the long bank and amid the shallow currents of the bridge', 'wading and delving', 'his stockings folded in his pockets and his canvas shoes dangling by their knotted laces over his shoulders', 'picking a pointed salteaten stick out of the jetsam among the rocks', 'down the slope of the breakwater', 'beneath the current swaying and turning'.

This passage occurs near the end of James Joyce's autobiographical novel *Portrait of the Artist as a Young Man*. Studied in its context, we see that it is of crucial importance. The hero has passed through an emotional struggle in which his new desire for freedom and adventure has been warring against the firmly established influences of home, country, and religion. He has reached the moment of decision when he knows that he must leave Ireland and go to the Continent, and this is the reason for the sense of exhilaration which possesses him as he wanders on the seashore near Dublin. The turning tide has become symbolic, like that

> tide in the affairs of men,
> Which, taken at the flood, leads on to fortune

which Shakespeare speaks of in *Julius Caesar*.

8

QUOTATION
20

'Yes, of course, if it's fine to-morrow,' said Mrs. Ramsay. 'But you'll have to be up with the lark,' she added.

To her son these words conveyed an extraordinary joy, as if it were settled the expedition were bound to take place, and the wonder to which he had looked forward, for years and years it seemed, was, after a night's darkness and a day's sail, within touch. Since he belonged, even at the age of six, to that great clan which cannot keep this feeling separate from that, but must let future prospects, with their joys and sorrows, cloud what is actually at hand, since to such people even in earliest childhood any turn in the wheel of sensation has the power to crystallise and transfix the moment upon which its gloom or radiance rests, James Ramsay, sitting on the floor cutting out pictures from the illustrated catalogue of the Army and Navy Stores, endowed the picture of a refrigerator as his mother spoke with heavenly bliss. It was fringed with joy. The wheelbarrow, the lawn-mower, the sound of poplar trees, leaves whitening before rain, rooks cawing, brooms knocking, dresses rustling— all these were so coloured and distinguished in his mind that he had already his private code, his secret language, though he appeared the image of stark and uncompromising severity, with his high forehead and his fierce blue eyes, impeccably candid and pure, frowning slightly at the sight of human frailty, so that his mother, watching him guide his scissors neatly round the refrigerator, imagined him all red and ermine on the Bench or directing a stern and momentous enterprise in some crisis of public affairs.

'But,' said his father, stopping in front of the drawing-room window, 'it won't be fine.'

Had there been an axe handy, a poker, or any weapon that would have gashed a hole in his father's breast and killed him, there and then, James would have seized it. Such were the extremes of emotion that Mr. Ramsay excited in his children's breasts by his mere presence; standing, as now, lean as a knife, narrow as the blade of one, grinning sarcastically, not only with the pleasure of disillusioning his son and casting ridicule upon his wife, who was ten thousand times better in every way than he was (James thought), but also with some secret conceit at his own accuracy of judgment. What he said was true. It was always true. He was incapable of untruth; never tampered with a fact; never altered a disagreeable word to suit the pleasure or convenience of any mortal being, least of all of his own children, who, sprung from his loins, should be aware from childhood that life is difficult; facts uncompromising; and the passage to that fabled land where our brightest hopes are extinguished, our frail barks founder in darkness (here Mr. Ramsay would straighten his back and narrow his little blue eyes upon the horizon), one that needs, above all, courage, truth, and the power to endure.

VIRGINIA WOOLF

In this passage the narrative is interwoven with psychological analysis and speculation to an extreme degree. It is the opening of Virginia Woolf's novel *To the Lighthouse*; the author is concerned, at the outset, with creating the right atmosphere and laying the foundations of the characters.

In the first paragraph we are told that there is to be an expedition if it is fine—an expedition to which the boy, James Ramsay, is passionately looking forward. We are also introduced to Mrs. Ramsay, who has a mother's ambitious dreams for her son. There is a bond of sympathy between mother and son, since both are of the kind to whom anticipation is all-important, and who 'must let future prospects, with their joys and sorrows, cloud what is actually at hand'.

In the third paragraph we are introduced to Mr. Ramsay, a man whose cold, logical, uncompromising regard for truth exasperates, and at times infuriates, his wife and children. Illusion, self-deception, and wishful thinking are the self-indulgent fancies which ordinary humans like the boy and his mother entertain. But Mr. Ramsay will have none of them. Ruthlessly he brushes them aside: 'But it won't be fine,' he taunts, and James is possessed by a murderous fury. The expedition referred to is the subject of the book's title, *To the Lighthouse*, and its importance is thus established right at the beginning.

In this kind of writing, psychological speculation and the minute analysis of the characters' states of mind are more important than narrative. In the second paragraph there is only one short sentence, in marked contrast to the immensely lengthy sentence which follows it. This final sentence of the second paragraph, although consisting of 105 words, contains only four clauses; these are amplified by the inclusion of the list beginning with 'The wheelbarrow', the appositional phrase 'his secret language', descriptive phrases such as 'with his high forehead', etc., participial expressions like 'frowning slightly', etc., and 'watching him guide his scissors', etc., and the alternative 'or directing a stern and momentous enterprise', etc. The style therefore tends to be a rambling series of phrases and expressions loosely strung together, with a minimum of finite verbs. It is especially adapted for rendering the loosely connected, unhurrying impressions and sensations which flow through the mind.

This rambling, reflective style in which the exploration of the characters' states of mind is more important than the relation of facts, is one of the most notable characteristics of early twentieth-century fiction and has left its mark on most fiction since. It was perhaps Laurence Sterne, author of *Tristram Shandy* and *A Sentimental Journey* in the middle of the eighteenth century, who originated this type of modern fiction; but its most considerable exponent was Henry James, whose influence on Virginia Woolf is obvious. Here are a few lines from *The Turn of the Screw* (1898) for comparison. They are supposed to be written by a governess just appointed to educate a little girl at her parents' country house.

QUOTATION
21

... I arranged with her, to her great satisfaction, that it should be she, she only, who might show me the place. She showed it step by step and room by room and secret by secret with droll, delightful, childish talk about it, and with the result, in half an hour, of our becoming tremendous friends. Young as she was, I was struck, through our little tour, with her confidence and courage, with the way, in empty chambers and dull corridors, on crooked stairways that made me pause, and even on the summit of an old machicolated square tower that made me dizzy, her morning music, her disposition to tell me so many more things than she asked, rang out and led me on. I have not seen Bly since the day I left it, and I daresay that to my present older and more informed eyes it would show a very reduced importance. But as my little conductress, with her hair of gold and her frock of blue, danced before me round corners and pattered down passages, I had the view of a castle of romance inhabited by a rosy sprite, such a place as would somehow for diversion of the young idea, take all colour out of story-books and fairy-tales. Wasn't it just a story-book over which I had fallen a-doze and a-dream? No; it was a big, ugly, antique but convenient house, embodying a few features of a building still older, half-displaced and half-utilised, in which I had the fancy of our being almost as lost as a handful of passengers in a great drifting ship. Well, I was strangely at the helm!

9

We described the style of Mungo Park as 'masculine'. Park was a doctor and an explorer. The masculine quality of his writing is connected with the active character of his life. If there is a corresponding 'feminine' kind of writing, we should expect it to arise from the traditionally less active nature of the lives of women. Where a man may explore or make speeches in public, a woman of intelligence may— until recently—have had to remain content with observation and silent comment. In literature, as we have seen in Quota-tion 20, a woman writer may excel in the analysis of character and situation. Compare the following quotation from Jane Austen:

QUOTATION
22

In the evening, as Marianne was discovered to be musical she was invited to play. The instrument was unlocked, every-body prepared to be charmed, and Marianne, who sang very well, at their request went through the chief of the songs which Lady Middleton had brought into the family on her marriage, and which had perhaps lain ever since in the same position on the pianoforte; for her ladyship had celebrated the event by giving up music, although by her mother's account she had played extremely well, and by her own was very fond of it.

Marianne's performance was highly applauded. Sir John was loud in his admiration at the end of every song, and as loud in his conversation with the others while every song lasted. Lady Middleton frequently called him to order, wondered how any one's attention could be diverted from music for a moment, and asked Marianne to sing a particular song which Marianne had just finished.

JANE AUSTEN

Sir John and Lady Middleton are host and hostess at a party at which Marianne was invited to sing, as was the custom in Jane Austen's time. Sir John reveals himself as being quite insensible to music, though he performs his duties as a host with enthusiasm; his wife reproves him for his inattention, but shows that she herself has not been listening either. The songs which she possessed on marriage have lain ever since untouched on the piano; singing was evidently one of her 'accomplishments' as a young lady—one for which her mother had been accustomed to praise her. Lady Middleton herself claims to be fond of music, but shows that she has no higher use for it than as a social grace.

Jane Austen is here satirizing cultural humbug among the polite people of her day. Her weapon is irony. She and Swift—two writers utterly different in most respects—are perhaps the greatest ironists in English. But whereas Swift's irony is savage and destructive, Jane Austen's is gentler and keener. Irony, which consists in saying the opposite of what you mean or of implying disapproval while you appear to approve, is the weapon of the intelligent obliged to associate with the foolish or barbarous. It enables him to maintain his own private standards while appearing to conform to those of society. It enables him to criticize without this being apparent to those he does not wish to offend. It is not altogether an admirable practice: the ironist has an air of superiority. But it may be his only method of retaining reason and sanity.

Jane Austen was a young woman of great intelligence and artistic sensibility condemned by circumstances to live in a more or less foolish and philistine, though good-hearted society. Under cover of her ever-polite but ever-vigilant irony she was able to criticize society and yet live with it, to retain her own artistic sensibility in detachment from her insensitive neighbours.

What delights us in this brief comment on Sir John and Lady Middleton is the cool and offhand way in which she disposes of their musical pretensions without for a moment losing her temper or her sense of fun. Moreover, her irony flatters the reader like a secret glance of understanding.

There are many types of irony, satire, and humour. To analyse them all would require a volume. Swift's irony, unlike Jane Austen's, is rarely humorous; the satirical purpose is too strong. But Jane Austen is more interested in extracting entertainment from society than in reforming it. The humour of the nineteenth-century American, Mark Twain, springs not from any deeply satirical motive but from the incongruities and absurdities of ordinary life. The following description of art in a genteel home, supposed to be written by Huckleberry Finn, an uneducated boy from a poor home, will serve as an example. The humour lies not only in the descriptions of the pictures themselves, which were evidently absurd enough, but also in the pathetically serious attitude of the boy towards his first experience of high art.

QUOTATION

23

They had pictures hung on the wall—mainly Washingtons and Lafayettes, and battles, and Highland Marys, and one called

'Signing the Declaration'. There was some that they called crayons, which one of their daughters which was dead made her own self when she was only fifteen years old. They was different from any pictures I ever seen before; blacker, mostly, than is common. One was a woman in a slim black dress, belted small under arm-pits, with bulges like a cabbage in the middle of the sleeves, and a large black scoop-shovel bonnet with a black veil, and white slim ankles crossed about with black tape, and very wee black slippers, like a chisel, and she was leaning pensive on a tombstone on her right below, under a weeping willow, and her other hand hanging down her side holding a white handkerchief and a reticule, and underneath the picture it said, 'Shall I Never See Thee More Alas?' Another one was a young lady with her hair all combed up straight to the top of her head, and knotted there in front of a comb like a chair-back, and she was crying into a handkerchief and had a dead bird laying on its back in her other hand with its heels up, and underneath the picture it said, 'I Shall Never Hear Thy Sweet Chirrup More Alas!' There was one where a young lady was at a window looking up at the moon, and tears running down her cheeks; and she had an open letter in one hand with black sealing-wax showing on one edge of it, and she was mashing a locket with a chain to it against her mouth, and underneath the picture it said, 'And Art Thou Gone Yes Thou Art Gone Alas!' These was all nice pictures, I reckon, but I didn't somehow seem to take to them, because if ever I was down a little, they always give me the fan-tods. Everybody was sorry she died, because she had laid out a lot more of these pictures to do, and a body could see by what she had done what they had lost. But I reckoned, that with her disposition, she was having a better time in the graveyard. She was at work on what they said was her greatest picture when she took sick, and every day and every night it was her prayer to be allowed to live till she had got it done, but she never got the chance. It was a picture of a young woman in a long white gown, standing on the rail of a bridge all ready to jump off, with her hair all down her back, and looking up to the moon, with the tears running down her face, and she had two arms folded across her breast, and two arms stretched out in front, and two more reaching up towards the moon—and the idea was, to see which pair would look best and then scratch out all the other arms; but, as I was a saying, she died before she got her mind made up, and now they kept this picture over the head of the bed in her room, and every time her birthday come they hung flowers on it. Other times it was hid with a little curtain. The young woman in the picture had a kind of a nice sweet face, but there was so many arms it made her look too spidery, seemed to me.

MARK TWAIN

10

We said at the beginning of this chapter that readers would not trouble to read the writings of an author whose grammar, sentence-construction, and word-order did not conform with the accepted usage of his time. There are sometimes exceptions. The early years of the twentieth century were a time of formal experimentation in all the arts. 'Modernism' in poetry, drama, painting, sculpture, architecture, and music took the form of a breaking away from accepted 'rules' and practice. In prose fiction, the most considerable experimenter was James Joyce. From his earliest to his latest work his style departs further and further from accepted conventions. In Quotation 19 we studied a paragraph from a fairly early book, where his style was more or less traditional. Let us conclude this chapter by looking at his later style.

QUOTATION

24

This way to the museyroom. Mind your hats goan in! Now yis are in the Willingdone Museyroom. This is a Prooshious gunn. This is a ffrinch. Tip. This is the flag of the Prooshious, the Cap and Soracer. This is the bullet that byng the flag of the

Prooshious. This is the ffrinch that fire on the Bull that bang the flag of the Prooshious. Saloos the Crossgunn! Up with your pike and fork! Tip. (Bullsfoot! Fine!) This is the triplewon hat of Lipoleum. Tip. Lipoleumhat. This is the Willingdone on his same white harse, the Cokenhape. This is the big Sraughter Willingdone, grand and magentic, in his gold-tin spurs and his ironed ducks and his quarterbrass woodyshoes and his magnate's gharters and his bangkok's best and goliar's goloshes and his pulluponeasyon wartrews. This is his big wide harse. Tip.

QUOTATION

25

Can't hear with the waters of. The chittering waters of. Flittering bats, fieldmice bawk talk. Ho! Are you not gone ahome? What Thom Malone? Can't hear the bawk of bats, all thim liffeying waters of. Ho, talk save us! My foos won't moos. I feel as old as yonder elm. A tale told of Shaun or Shem? All Livia's daughtersons. Dark hawks near us. Night! Night! My ho head halls. I feel as heavy as yonder stone. Tell me of John or Shaun? Who were Shem and Shaun the living sons or daughters of? Night now! Tell me, tell me, tell me, elm! Night night! Temetale of stem or stone. Beside the rivering waters of, hitherandthithering waters of. Night!

These two paragraphs are from James Joyce's final work, whose publication began in 1927 and finished with the completed novel, *Finnegan's Wake*, in 1939, two years before the author's death. At first sight it is an incomprehensible farrago, part sense and part nonsense; but careful study shows that the writing is deliberate, highly organized, and perfectly lucid, though difficult. Everyday language is broken up and reassembled to exploit its maximum allusive and suggestive possibilities. Puns and ellipses abound. Most readers find that the book requires too much concentration and ingenuity to be read in long stretches, but read in short passages it is brilliant and amusing. The style is too original to be imitated, and it is difficult to see how the experimental distortion of ordinary prose could be carried further.

In the first of these two paragraphs a garrulous guide conducts a tour through a historical museum. Various relics of the Napoleonic Wars are exhibited, including Wellington himself, the Irish-born victor of Waterloo on his white horse Copenhagen; a precious Prussian gun, and Napoleon's three-cornered hat. There are punning references to Admiral Byng, John Bull, the Iron Duke, Quatre Bras, Magna Carta, and Wellington boots (Goliath's goloshes).

The second paragraph is the final passage from an incident called *Anna Livia Plurabelle*, in which some gossiping washer-women are washing clothes in the River Liffey near Dublin. Livia stands for Liffey, mother of Ireland's sons, typified as Shaun and Shem (John and James). The speaker is dropping off to sleep, lulled by the sound of the river and the creatures of night. She feels as old, heavy, and rooted as the elms by the river. *Thom Malone* is a pun on 'home alone'; *bawk* contains suggestions of 'bawdry' and 'baulk'; *my foos won't moos* is a drowsy corruption of 'my foot won't move'; Shem or Shaun becomes *stem or stone*.

A reader who finds this merely ingenious misses its beauty: just as the language seems to dissolve into drowsy incoherence, so does the speaker (or speakers), under the influence of sleep and weariness, seem to melt into the very earth and roots of the riverside scene. This is as moving and tender as anything in modern Irish literature.

II

We have now examined critically a number of examples of English prose and should be in a position to draw some general conclusions which may be helpful in examining others.

One of the first things we are likely to notice is whether the style is clear or obscure. If we find a writer obscure, it may be because his style is slipshod or hasty, or it may be because he has something difficult to say. In that case, the fault may be ours; perhaps we should be reading with closer attention.

If on the other hand, we find the style clear and easy to follow at a fair speed, we shall then go on to notice whether the writing is objective or subjective. This appears to be one of the main distinctions to be made in criticizing prose. An objective writer is one whose personality is kept in the background; we may get an impression of the quality of his intellect, his power of mind, but we shall not get a clear impression of his private personality. This is something we derive from the reading of subjective prose—prose marked throughout by touches which give away the writer's tastes and temperament. An objective writer appears to write authoritatively, as if what he says is true, independently of his personal impressions. A subjective writer makes no attempt to keep his personal impressions to himself; he shows clearly that he is writing of things as seen through his eyes; and how they appear will differ according to his moods. On the whole, scientific or factual writing is usually of an objective kind; memoirs, personal narratives and imaginative writing are often subjective. We read the former kind of writing for what it has to say; we read the second kind more for an impression of the writer's personality.

Objective narrative is factual, objective description we call realistic; subjective description we call impressionistic. The former appears more solid, like the seventeenth-century domestic scenes painted by the Dutch school; the latter is more vague, but often more lifelike, and may be compared with the pictures of the nineteenth-century French painters known as Impressionists. Both sorts of writing have their place in literature.

Sometimes, of course, a writer uses a blend of objective and subjective writing, realism and impressionism. The English novel, for instance, from Defoe to Virginia Woolf, has on the whole tended to move away from realism and towards impressionism; psychological analysis of character, while expressed in objective terms, is necessarily of a partly subjective nature, since a novelist cannot be strictly factual about what goes on from moment to moment in other people's minds.

We may sometimes say of objective writing that it is detached and unemotional; subjective writing is often emotional. The ironist writes in a detached way; he stands apart from his subject. His emotions are kept below the surface. On the other hand, the subdued emotion may break through to the surface and express itself in the form of ridicule or indignation. One of the points to notice about prose writing is the writer's emotional attitude to his subject—whether the emotion is present or absent, and if present, whether it is below the surface, betraying itself only by an occasional adjective, or whether it is near the surface, ready to communicate itself at any moment directly to the reader.

We have spoken of 'masculine' and 'feminine' writing; this implies no absolute distinction, nor does it relate invariably to the writing of men and women respectively. A masculine style is direct, sometimes crude, sometimes pompous or dogmatic, full of strong light and shade, concrete, and not emotionally subtle; a feminine style is more subtle in emotion and observation, full of suggestion and half-lights, less forceful. It need hardly be said that the most interesting writing, like the most interesting characters, contains both masculine and feminine qualities. An excessively masculine style wearies by being too forceful; an excessively feminine style irritates by its suggestion of niggling fussiness.

Another distinction we shall make in examining prose style is that between the experimental and the traditional. The majority of prose writers are conservative in style, conforming to accepted patterns of sentence structure and choice of words. At certain periods, however, as during the Elizabethan age or during the 1920's, there has been a marked tendency to experiment with original word patterns. A writer has something new to say and he feels impelled to say it in a self-consciously new way. When we read experimental prose, we must decide whether the writer really has anything new to say or whether he is only striving for effect. To some extent, of course, every truly original writer develops his personal style and departs, however slightly, from accepted usage. But paradoxically every great and original writer is at the same time experimental and traditional. Swift, Burke, Hazlitt, Borrow, James—all are original, personal, yet all are traditional, all wrote in the style of their time. This is because the truly great writers *create* the style of their time; it is not until afterwards that we can see that they have done this. In reading the prose writings of our own day, we may wonder which of them have created, or are creating, the style of their time, the style by which the twentieth century will be recognized in future times.

In coming closer to a prose passage and examining it in greater detail, the first thing we shall probably be aware of is the vocabulary, the choice of word and phrase. We shall notice slang, uneducated forms, archaic words, learned or literary allusions, hackneyed or outworn expressions. These we shall comment on as they affect the writer's general intention. If he is trying to suggest the thoughts of an ordinary person in a colloquial way, slang will not be out of place, where learned or archaic words would. Technical terms in, for instance, architecture would be suitable where the writer wanted to dwell on a particular building in its historical setting. An excess of adjectives will weaken the general effect of a passage, particularly if the adjectives are commonplace or hackneyed. On the other hand, an excessive seeking for new and strange words will weary and irritate the reader.

When we come to consider these words in combination, we shall notice first the general rhythm or flow of the passage. If it is jerky, this may be from deliberate intention. Before condemning a style for jerkiness, we must see whether this has any deliberate purpose. The fashion in sentence lengths changes from time to time, like that in dresses. On the whole, the tendency in English, as it got further and further away from Latin models and developed its own character, has been away from long sentences. What we should consider a long sentence in a modern novelist would not have been considered long in Fielding or Dr. Johnson. What we have to notice in this respect is whether there is sufficient variety; a certain degree of variety is essential if interest is to be maintained.

Sentences of complicated grammatical construction, with many dependent and sub-dependent clauses, make the sense difficult to follow. There may be justification if the writer has something really involved and difficult to say.

Word-order is another important aspect of style. The most effective writers in English are those who have mastered this extremely difficult technique. In English, sense is often determined directly by word-order, because we have no inflections. If we wish to say that a dog chases a man, we must put the words 'dog' and 'man' in that order, unless we alter the form of the verb. This appears obvious; but it is not so in Latin—the Romans could put the man first for the sake of emphasis, and the inflected word-endings would make the sense clear. Position in English, however, determines not only sense, but also, to some extent, emphasis. The most emphatic positions are the beginning and end of a sentence —particularly the end, since that is where we pause before starting the next sentence. The most effective writer is the one who can best balance the needs of sense and of emphasis keeping the word-order as natural as possible while getting the emphatic word or phrase as often as possible to the end of the sentence. It was because he was able to do this supremely well that the dramatic prose of Bernard Shaw was so telling and effective. An earlier writer whose mastery of word-order is worth study is Lord Macaulay.

Clarity is the great objective in prose writing—the quality of saying exactly what is intended as unmistakably and simply as possible, without false emphasis or straining after effect. Indeed, we might say—and it is another of the paradoxes of literary criticism—that the great aim of style is to divert attention from itself and towards the subject. To criticize, we must make ourselves aware of the means by which a writer succeeds or fails; but to enjoy his work fully, we should be as little as possible aware of his style. If we are continually interested, moved, and excited by what we read, then the writer is doing his work successfully. If we are for ever stopping to think what he means, or if we are, so to speak, forced to admire his style, he is not writing well. Yet if our taste is bad, we shall be stirred by inferior writing; that is why we must sometimes stop to criticize. The improvement of our taste is the justification of criticism.

PROSE PASSAGES FOR CRITICISM

(Names of authors given at end of Chapter, page 67)

I

'It is late,' I heard her whisper. 'It will be dark in the plantation.' She shook my arm, and repeated, 'Marion! it will be dark in the plantation.'

'Give me a minute longer,' I said—'a minute, to get better in.'

I was afraid to trust myself to look at her yet; and I kept my eyes fixed on the view.

It *was* late. The dense brown line of trees in the sky had faded in the gathering darkness, to the faint resemblance of a long wreath of smoke. The mist over the lake below had stealthily enlarged, and advanced cn us. The silence was as breathless as ever—but the horror of it had gone, and the solemn mystery of its stillness was all that remained.

'We are far from the house,' she whispered. 'Let us go back.'

She stopped suddenly, and turned her face from me towards the entrance of the boat-house.

'Marion!' she said, trembling violently. 'Do you see nothing? Look!'

'Where?'

'Down there, below us.'

She pointed. My eyes followed her hand; and I saw it too.

A living figure was moving over the waste of heath in the distance. It crossed our range of view from the boat-house, and passed darkly along the outer edge of the mist. It stopped far off, in front of us—waited—and passed on, moving slowly, with the white cloud of mist behind it and above it—slowly, slowly, till it glided by the edge of the boat-house, and we saw it no more.

We were both unnerved by what had passed between us that evening. Some minutes elapsed before Laura would venture into the plantation, and before I could make up my mind to lead her back to the house.

2

To recline on a stump of thorn in the central valley of Egdon, between afternoon and night, as now, where the eye could reach nothing of the world outside the summits and shoulders of heathland which filled the whole circumference of its glance, and to know that everything around and underneath had been from prehistoric times as unaltered as the stars overhead, gave ballast to the mind adrift on change, and harassed by the irrepressible New. The great inviolate place had an ancient permanence which the sea cannot claim. Who can say of a particular sea that it is old? Distilled by the sun, kneaded by the moon, it is renewed in a year, in a day, or in an hour. The sea changed, the fields changed, the rivers, the villages, and the people changed, yet Egdon remained. Those surfaces were neither so steep as to be destructible by weather, nor so flat as to be the victims of floods and deposits. With the exception of an aged highway, and a still more aged barrow presently to be referred to—themselves almost crystallised to natural products by long continuance—even the trifling irregularities were not caused by pickaxe, plough, or spade, but remained as the very finger-touches of the last geological change.

3

After two days' tedious journey, it was refreshing to see in the distance the rows of poplars and willows growing round the village of Luxan. Shortly before we arrived at this place we observed to the south a ragged cloud of a dark reddish-brown colour. At first we thought that it was smoke from some great fire on the plains; but we soon found that it was a swarm of locusts. They were flying northward; and with the aid of a light breeze, they overtook us at a rate of ten or fifteen miles an hour. The main body filled the air from a height of twenty feet, to that, as it appeared, of two or three thousand above the ground; and the sound of their wings was as the sound of chariots of many horses running to battle; or rather, I should say, like a strong breeze passing through the rigging of a ship. The sky, seen through the advanced guard, appeared like a mezzotinto engraving, but the main body was impervious to sight; they were not, however, so thick together, but they could escape a stick waved backwards and forwards. When they alighted, they were more numerous than the leaves in the field, and the surface became reddish instead of being green: the swarm having once alighted, the individuals flew from side to side in all directions. Locusts are not an uncommon pest in this country: already during this season, several smaller swarms had come up from the south, where, as apparently in all other parts of the world, they are bred in the deserts. The poor cottagers in vain attempted, by lighting fires, by shouts, and by waving branches to avert the attack.

4

Once, when clambering among the rough rocks, overgrown with forest, among the Queneveta mountains, I came on a single white flower which was new to me, which I have never seen since. After I had looked long at it, and passed on, the image of that perfect flower remained so persistently in my mind that on the following day I went again, in the hope of seeing it still untouched by decay. There was no change; and on this occasion I spent a much longer time looking at it, admiring the marvellous beauty of its form, which seemed so greatly to exceed that of all other flowers. It had thick petals, and at first gave me the idea of an artificial flower, cut by a divinely inspired artist from some unknown precious stone, of the size of a large orange and whiter than milk, and yet, in spite of its opacity, with a crystalline lustre on the surface. Next day I went again, scarcely hoping to find it still unwithered; it was fresh as if only just opened; and after that I went often, sometimes at intervals of several days, and still no faintest sign of any change, the clear, exquisite lines still undimmed, the purity and lustre as I had first seen it. Why, I often asked, does not this mystic forest flower fade and perish like others? That first impression of its artificial appearance had soon left me; it was, indeed, a flower, and, like other flowers, had life and growth, only with that transcendant beauty it had a different kind of life. Unconscious, but higher; perhaps immortal. Thus it would continue to bloom when I had looked my last on it; wind and rain and sunlight would never stain, never tinge, its sacred purity; the savage Indian, though he sees little to admire in a flower, yet seeing this one would veil his face and turn back; even the browsing beast crashing his way though the forest, struck with its strange glory, would swerve aside and pass on without harming it. Afterwards I heard from some Indians, to whom I described it, that the flower I had discovered was called Hata; also that they had a superstition concerning it—a strange belief. They said that only one Hata flower existed in the world; that it bloomed in one spot for the space of a moon; that on the disappearance of the moon in the sky the Hata disappeared from its place, only to reappear blooming in some other spot, sometimes in some distant forest. And they also said that whosoever discovered the Hata flower in the forest would overcome all his enemies and obtain all his desires, and finally outlive other men by many years. But, as I have said, all this I heard afterwards, and my half-superstitious feeling for the flower had grown up independently in my own mind.

5

... It was the hour and the season in which the Bois seems, perhaps, most multiform, not only because it is then most divided, but because it is divided in a different way. Even in the unwooded parts, where the horizon is large, here and there against the background of a dark and distant mass of trees, now leafless or still keeping their summer foliage unchanged, a double row of orange-red chestnuts seemed, as in a picture just begun, to be the only thing painted, so far, by an artist who had not yet laid any colour on the rest, and to be offering their cloister, in full daylight, for the casual exercise of the human figures that would be added to the picture later on.

Farther off, at a place where the trees were still all green, one alone, small, stunted, lopped, but stubborn in its resistance, was tossing in the breeze an ugly mane of red. Elsewhere, again, might be seen the first awakening of this Maytime of the leaves, and those of an ampelopsis, a smiling miracle, like a red hawthorn flowering in the winter, had that very morning all 'come out', so to speak, in blossom. And the Bois had the temporary, unfinished, artificial look of a nursery garden or a park in which, either for some botanic purpose or in preparation for a festival, there had been embedded among the trees of commoner growth, which have not yet been uprooted and transplanted elsewhere, a few rare specimens, with fantastic foliage, which seem to be clearing all round themselves an empty space, making room, giving air, diffusing light. Thus it was the time of year at which the Bois de Boulogne displays more separate characteristics, assembles more distinct elements in a composite whole than at any other.

6

... I like catching the 2.40; I like the slow, smooth roll of the great big trains—and they are the best trains in the world! I like being drawn through the green country and looking at it through the clear glass of the great windows. Though, of course, the country isn't really green. The sun shines, the earth is blood red and purple and red and green and red. And the oxen in the plough-lands are bright varnished brown and black and blackish purple; and the peasants are dressed in the black and white of magpies; and there are great flocks of magpies too. Or the peasants' dresses in another field where there are little mounds of hay that will be grey-green on the sunny side and purple in the shadow—the peasants' dresses are vermilion with emerald green ribbons and purple skirts and white shirts and black velvet stomachers. Still, the impression is that you are drawn through brilliant green meadows that run away on each side to the dark purple fir-woods; the basalt pinnacles; the immense forests. And there is meadow-sweet at the edge of the streams, and cattle. Why, I remember on that afternoon I saw a brown cow hitch its horns under the stomach of a black and white animal and the black and white one was thrown right into the middle of a narrow stream. I burst out laughing.... I chuckled over it from time to time for the whole rest of the day. Because it does look very funny, you know, to see a black and white cow land on its back in the middle of a stream. It is so just exactly what one doesn't expect of a cow.

I suppose I ought to have pitied the poor animal; but I just didn't. I was out for enjoyment. And I just enjoyed myself. It is so pleasant to be drawn along in front of the spectacular towns with the peaked castles and the many double spires. In the sunlight gleams come from the city—gleams from the glass of the windows; from the gilt signs of apothecaries; from the ensigns of the student corps high up in the mountains; from the helmets of the funny little soldiers moving their stiff little legs in white linen trousers. And it was pleasant to get out in the great big spectacular Prussian station with the hammered bronze ornaments and the paintings of peasants and flowers and cows.

7

The towers of Zenith aspired above the morning mist; austere towers of steel and cement and limestone, sturdy as cliffs and delicate as silver rods. They were neither citadels nor churches, but frankly and beautifully office-buildings.

The mist took pity on the fretted structures of earlier generations: the Post Office with its shingle-tortured mansard, the red brick minarets of hulking old houses, factories with stingy and sooted windows, wooden tenements covered with mud. The city was full of such grotesqueries, but the clean towers were thrusting them from the business centre, and on the farther hills were shining new houses, homes—they seemed—for laughter and tranquillity.

Over a concrete bridge fled a limousine of long sleek hood and noiseless engine. These people in evening clothes were returning from an all-night rehearsal of a Little Theatre play, an artistic adventure considerably illuminated by champagne. Below the bridge curved a railway, a maze of green and crimson lights. The New York Flier boomed past, and twenty lines of polished steel leaped into the glare.

In one of the skyscrapers the wires of the Associated Press were being closed. The telegraph operators wearily raised their celluloid eye-shades after a night of talking to Paris and Peking. Through the building crawled the charwomen, yawning, their old shoes slapping. The dawn mist spun away. Queues of men with lunch-boxes clumped towards the immensity of new factories, sheets of glass and hollow tile, glittering shops where five thousand men worked beneath one roof, pouring out the honest wares that would be sold up the Euphrates and across the Veldt. The whistles rolled out in greeting a chorus cheerful as the April dawn; the song of labour in a city built—it seemed—for giants.

8

What is strangest is that he carries this sentiment into classical subjects, its most complete expression being a picture in the *Uffizi*, of Venus rising from the sea, in which the grotesque emblems of the middle age, and a landscape full of its peculiar feeling, and even its strange draperies, powdered all over in the Gothic manner with a quaint conceit of daisies, frame a figure that reminds you of the faultless nude studies of Ingres. At first, perhaps, you are attracted only by a quaintness of design, which seems to recall all at once whatever you have read of Florence in the fifteenth century; afterwards you may think that this quaintness must be incongruous with the subject, and that the colour is cadaverous or at least cold. And yet, the more you come to understand what imaginative colouring really is, that all colour is no mere delightful quality of natural things, but a spirit upon them by which they become expressive to the spirit, the better you will like this peculiar quality of colour; and you will find that quaint design of Botticelli's a more direct inlet into the greek temper than the works of the Greeks themselves even of the finest period. . . . The light is indeed cold—mere sunless dawn; but a later painter would have cloyed you with sunshine; and you can see the better for that quietness in the morning air each long promontory, as it slopes down to the water's edge. Men go forth to their labours until the evening; but she is awake before them, and you might think that the sorrow in her face was at the thought of the whole long day of love yet to come. An emblematical figure of the wind blows hard across the grey water, moving forward the dainty-lipped shell on which she sails, the sea 'showing his teeth', as it moves, in thin lines of foam, and sucking in, one by one, the falling roses, each severe in outline, plucked off short at the stalk, but embrowned a little, as Botticelli's flowers always are. Botticelli meant all this imagery to be altogether pleasurable; and it was partly an incompleteness of resources, inseparable from the art of that time, that subdued and chilled it. But this predilection for minor tones counts also; and what is unmistakable is the sadness with which he has conceived the goddess of pleasure, as the depository of a great power over the lives of men.

9

The house in which I live is haunted by the noise of dripping water. Always, day and night, summer and winter, something is dripping somewhere. For many months an unquiet cistern kept up within its iron bosom a long, hollow-toned soliloquy. Now it is mute; but a new and more formidable drip has come into existence. From the very summit of the house a little spout—the overflow, no doubt, of some unknown receptacle under the roof—lets fall a succession of drips that is almost a continuous stream. Down it falls, this all but stream, a sheer forty or fifty feet on to the stones of the basement steps, thence to dribble ignominiously away into some appointed drain. The cataracts blow their trumpets from the steep; but my lesser waterfalls play a subtler, I had almost said a more 'modern' music. Lying awake at nights, I listen with a mixture of pleasure and irritation to its curious cadences.

10

How to get senior value at junior prices

Keeping a teen-ager sartorially up to snuff was once a pain in the pocketbook.

But that was before the biggest innovation in years hit the boys'-wear markets. *Rayon was adapted to fit the requirements of year-round wear!*

Just as manufacturers and cooperating research men made rayon crisply cool for summer, they developed rayon fabrics with air-trapping, warmth-retaining constructions for the cooler months. Some are 100% rayon and are completely mothproof. Others are blends of rayon and wool. Being wrinkle-resistant, they fit right into a boy's life.

And best of all these superior fabrics could be handsomely tailored into sturdy, good-looking suits and slacks that are priced well within the range of most family budgets.

These garments are waiting to take your son back to school now. You'll find them in your favorite shop.

11

... Ata's house stood about eight kilometres from the road that runs round the island, and you went to it along a winding pathway shaded by luxuriant trees of the tropics. It was a bungalow of unpainted wood, consisting of two small rooms, and outside was a small shed that served as a kitchen. There was no furniture except the mats they used as beds and a rocking chair, which stood on the verandah. Bananas with their great ragged leaves, like the tattered habiliments of an empress in adversity, grew close up to the house. There was a tree just behind which bore alligator pears, and all about were the coconuts which gave the island its revenue. Ata's father had planted crotons round his property, and they grew in coloured profusion, gay and brilliant; they fenced the land with flame. A mango grew in front of the house, and at the edge of the clearing were two flamboyants, twin trees, that challenged the gold of the coconuts with their scarlet flowers.

12

What a figure! He was about forty years of age, and his height might have amounted to some six feet two inches, had he not been curved much after the fashion of the letter S. No weasel ever appeared lanker, and he looked as if a breath of air would have been sufficient to blow him away. His face might certainly have been called handsome, had it not been for its extraordinary and portentous meagreness; his nose was like an eagle's bill, his teeth white as ivory, his eyes black—oh, how black!—and fraught with a strange expression; his skin was dark, and the hair of his head like the plumage of the raven. A deep quiet smile dwelt continually on his features; but with all the quiet it was a cruel smile, such a one as would have graced the countenance of a Nero.

13

The nomads' camels are strong and frolic in these fat weeks of the spring pasture. Now it is they lay up flesh, and grease in their humps, for the languor of the desert summer and the long year. Driven home full-bellied at sunset, they come hugely bouncing in before their herdsmen: the householders, going forth from the booths, lure to them as they run lurching by, with loud *Wolloo-wolloo-wolloo*, and to stay them *Woh-ho, wòh-ho, wòh-ho!* they chide any that strikes a tent-cord with *hutch!* The camels are couched every troop beside, about, and the more of them before the booth of their household; there all night they lie ruckling and chawing their huge cuds till the light of the morrow. The Arabs say that their camels never sleep; the weary brute may stretch down his long neck upon the ground, closing awhile his great liquid eyes; but after a space he will right again the great languid carcase and fall to chawing. In this fresh season they rise to graze anew in the moonlight, and roam from the booths of the slumbering Arab; but fearful by nature, they stray not then very far off.

14

Of all the creatures of commercial enterprise, the canal barge is by far the most delightful to consider. It may spread its sails, and then you see it sailing high above the tree-tops and the windmill, sailing on the aqueduct, sailing through the green corn-lands: the most picturesque of things amphibious. Or the horse plods along at a footpace as if there were no such thing as business in the world; and the man dreaming at the tiller sees the same spire on the horizon all day long. It is a mystery how things ever get to their destination at this rate; and to see the barges waiting their turn at a lock, affords a fine lesson of how easily the world may be taken. There should be many contented spirits on board, for such a life is both to travel and to stay at home.

The chimney smokes for dinner as you go along; the banks of the canal slowly unroll their scenery to contemplative eyes; the barge floats by great forests and through great cities with their public buildings and their lamps at night; and for the bargee, in his floating home, 'travelling abed', it is merely as if he were listening to another man's story or turning the leaves of a picture book in which he had no concern. He may take his afternoon walk in some foreign country on the banks of the canal, and then come home to dinner at his own fireside.

15

It goes along like that for three rounds more. They don't talk any. They're working all the time. We worked over Jack plenty too, in between the rounds. He don't look good at all but he never does much work in the ring. He don't move around much and that left-hand is just automatic. It's just like it was connected with Walcott's face and Jack just had to wish it in every time. Jack is always calm in close and he doesn't waste any juice. He knows everything about working in close too and he's getting away with a lot of stuff. While they were in our corner I watched him tie Walcott up, get his right hand loose, turn it and come up with an uppercut that got Walcott's nose with the heel of the glove. Walcott was bleeding bad and leaned his nose on Jack's shoulder so as to give Jack some of it too, and Jack sort of lifted his shoulder sharp and caught him against the nose, and then brought down the right hand and did the same thing again.

Walcott was sore as hell. By the time they'd gone five rounds he hated Jack's guts. Jack wasn't sore; that is, he wasn't any sorer than he always was. He certainly did used to make the fellows he fought hate boxing. That was why he hated Richie Lewis so. He never got Richie's goat. Richie Lewis always had about three new dirty things Jack couldn't do. Jack was as safe as a church all the time he was in there as long as he was strong. He certainly was treating Walcott rough. The funny thing was it looked as though Jack was an open classic boxer. That was because he had all that stuff too.

16

She had the mouth that smiles in repose. The lips met full on the centre of the bow and thinned along to a lifting dimple; the eyelids also lifted slightly at the outer corners and seemed, like the lip into the limpid cheek, quickening up the temples, as with a run of light, or the ascension indicated off a shoot of colour. Her features were playfellows of one another, none of them pretending to rigid correctness, nor the nose to the ordinary dignity of governess among merry girls, despite which the nose was of a fair design, not acutely interrogative or inviting to gambols. Aspens imaged in water, waiting for the breeze, would offer a susceptible lover some suggestion of her face: a pure smooth white face, tenderly flushed in the cheeks, where the gentle dints were faintly inter-melting even during quietness. Her eyes were brown, set well between mild lids, often shadowed, not unwakeful. Her hair of lighter brown, swelling above her temples in the sweep to the knot, imposed the triangle of the fabulous wild woodland visage from brow to mouth and chin, evidently in agreement with her taste; and the triangle suited her; but her face was not significant of a tameless wildness or of weakness; the equitable shut mouth threw its long curve to guard the small round chin from that effect; her eyes wavered only in humour, they were steady when thoughtfulness was awakened; and at such seasons the build of her winter-beechwood hair lost the touch of nymph-like and whimsical, and strangely, by mere outline, added to her appearance a studious concentration.

17

... It was the same in the next round; but the balance of power was thus restored—the fate of the battle was suspended. No one could tell how it would end. This was the only moment in which opinion was divided; for, in the next, the Gas-man aiming a mortal blow at his adversary's neck, with his right hand, and failing from the length he had to reach, the other returned it with his left at full swing, planted a tremendous blow on his cheek-bone and eye-brow, and made a red ruin of that side of his face. The Gas-man went down, and there was another shout—a roar of triumph as the waves of fortune rolled tumultuously from side to side. This was a settler. Hickman got up, and 'grinned horrible a ghastly smile,' yet he was evidently dashed in his opinion of himself; it was the first time he had ever been so punished; all one side of his face was perfect scarlet, and his right eye was closed in dingy blackness, as he advanced to the fight, less confident, but still determined. After one or two rounds, not receiving another such remembrancer, he rallied and went at it with his former impetuosity. But in vain. His strength had been weakened,—his blows could not tell at such a distance,—he was obliged to fling himself at his adversary, and could not strike from his feet; and almost as regularly as he flew at him with his right hand, Neate warded the blow, or drew back out of its reach, and felled him with the return of his left. There was little cautious sparring—no half-hits—no tapping and trifling, none of the *petit-maitreship* of the art—they were almost all knock-down blows:—the fight was a good stand-up fight.

18

I had forgotten about his eyes. They were as blue as the sides of a certain type of box of matches. When you looked at them carefully, you saw that they were perfectly honest, perfectly straightforward, perfectly, perfectly stupid. But the brick pink of his complexion, running perfectly level to the brick pink of his inner eyelids, gave them a curious, sinister expression—like a mosaic of blue porcelain set in pink china. And that chap, coming into a room, snapped up the gaze of every woman in it, as dexterously as a conjurer pockets billiard balls. It was most amazing. You know the man on the stage who throws up sixteen balls at once and they all drop into pockets all over his person, on his shoulders, on his heels, on the inner side of his sleeves; and he stands perfectly still and does nothing. Well, it was like that. He had rather a rough, hoarse voice.

19

In a well mix'd Metropolitan Fog, there is something substantial and satisfying—you can feel what you breathe, and see it too. It is like breathing water, as we may fancy the fishes do. And then the taste of it, when dashed with a fine season of sea-coal smoke, is far from insipid.

It is also meat and drink at the same time; something between egg-flip and *Omelette souffle*; but much more digestible than either. Not that I would recommend it medicinally—especially to persons that have queasy stomachs, delicate nerves and afflicted with bile; but for persons of good robust habit of body, and not dainty withal (which such, by the way, never are), there is nothing better in its way. And it wraps you all round like a cloak, too—a patent waterproof one, which no rain ever penetrated. No; I maintain that a real London Fog is a thing not to be sneezed at—if you can help it.

20

Sharp showers, bright between. Late in the afternoon, the light and shade being brilliant, snowy blocks of cloud were filing over the sky, and under the sun hanging above and along the earth-line were those multitudinous up-and-down crispy sparkling chains with pearly shadows up to the edges. At sunset, which was in a grey bank with moist gold dabs and racks, the whole round of skyline had level clouds naturally lead-colour but the upper parts ruddled, some more, some less, rosy. Spits or beams braided or built in with slanting pellet flakes made their way. Through such clouds anvil-shaped pink ones and up-blown fleece-of-wool flat-topped dangerous-looking pieces.

SOURCES OF THE FOREGOING PROSE PASSAGES

1. Wilkie Collins, *The Woman in White*.
2. Thomas Hardy, *The Return of the Native*.
3. Charles Darwin, *The Voyage of the Beagle*.
4. W. H. Hudson, *Green Mansions*.
5. Marcel Proust, *Swann's Way* (translated by C. K. Scott Moncrieff).
6. Ford Madox Ford, *The Good Soldier*.
7. Sinclair Lewis, *Babbitt*.
8. Walter Pater, *The Renaissance*.
9. Aldous Huxley, *On the Margin* (essay on *Water Music*).
10. Anonymous, an American advertisement.
11. W. Somerset Maugham, *The Moon and Sixpence*.
12. George Borrow, *The Bible in Spain*.
13. Charles Doughty, *Arabia Deserta*.
14. R. L. Stevenson, *An Inland Voyage*.
15. Ernest Hemingway, *Men Without Women*.
16. George Meredith, *The Egoist*.
17. William Hazlitt, *The Fight*.
18. Ford Madox Ford, *The Good Soldier*.
19. Charles Lamb, *Essays and Sketches*.
20. G. M. Hopkins, *Journal, July 1st 1886*.

III

THE CRITICISM OF POETRY

I

Much of what has been said in a general way about prose applies in even greater degree to poetry. For the content-form paradox assumes striking importance. Content and form, or matter and style, are inseparable: you cannot alter the form or expression—the style—without altering the thing expressed—the matter of content. If this is true of prose, how much truer is it of poetry, in which, generally speaking, there is much tighter organization of form. The exigences of metre and rhyme make it even more impossible to alter the form without altering the content. The paradox is, however, that in criticism we do continually, and we must, speak of form and content as if they were separate things.

Suppose in a story for children we were to say, 'the death of the robin caused great unhappiness among the other birds.' This is not in itself poetry. But who can deny that the expression of the same idea in the old nursery rhyme is true poetry, by no means trivial and in fact rather moving—to children, very moving?

> All the birds of the air fell a-sighing and a-sobbing
> When they heard of the death of poor Cock Robin.

Now the death of a robin is in itself a moving event, at any rate to children. It might be said, therefore, that the nursery rhyme version is really no more poetic than the prose version, since the pathetic event is related in each, and it is the event which is moving. But in some way there is a shift in the reader's emotion when he turns from one version to the other; the pathos shifts, as it were, from the event to the form: in the prose version the pathos is in the event, in the poetic version it is in the words.

> *All* the birds of the air fell a-sighing and a-sobbing
> When they heard of the death of poor Cock Robin.

To begin with, there is the rhythm, with which is always associated heightened emotion. The rhythm is not in itself a sad rhythm, though the heavy accentuation here makes it possible to associate the rhythm with a feeling of sadness. Then there is the alliteration in 'a-sighing and a-sobbing'. There is also the direct suggestion of universal woe in the phrase 'All the birds of the air'; the sadness of the word 'fell'; and there is also the expression of sympathy in the commonplace word 'poor'. Perhaps, too, the rhyme strengthens the feeling, since it places emphasis on the final word 'Robin'.

We may say therefore that the nursery-rhyme version gives an emotional rendering of the event, in which feelings are aroused, not only by the event itself, but also by the form in which it is expressed. We can further give these formal effects their technical names of 'rhythm', 'rhyme', 'alliteration' and 'diction'. But we must guard against the temptation to talk about these effects in complete isolation. There is no such thing as 'rhythm'—there are only events in rhythm, of which words of course are in poetry all-important. There is no such thing as 'rhyme', only rhymed words or syllables. There is no such thing as 'alliteration', only words in alliteration. There is no such thing as 'diction' in the abstract; there is only the diction, the words, of a particular poem or a particular poet. These technical effects are abstractions drawn from actual poems. If we think of them as having an existence of their own, our criticism of poems will lack reality. It is common in literary text-books to treat of these effects or devices in isolation, with the intention of discovering them afterwards in poetical examples. This is to put the cart before the horse. We should always study actual poems, discovering if need be the presence of technical effects as contributing to the total effect. To say that Marlowe's *Tamburlaine* and Tennyson's *Idylls of the King* are both in blank verse; that Blake's *Auguries of Innocence* and Marvell's *To His Coy Mistress* are both in octosyllabic couplets; that Shakespeare's *Let me not to the marriage of true minds* and Wordsworth's *The world is too much with us* are both sonnets—this is to say nothing whatever about the poems themselves. The expressions 'blank verse', 'octosyllabic couplets', and 'sonnet' are technical terms in poetry, and are used simply as ways of describing form. The same is true of terms such as 'metaphor', 'simile', 'onomatopoeia', 'assonance' and the like. These are the vocabulary of description, they do not contain critical ideas. Yet it is sometimes thought that to acquire and use this vocabulary has something to do with the criticism of poetry. It has very little. It is useful to know these words, because they are abbreviations for otherwise lengthy descriptions. But to learn them *first* is a mistake. They do not in themselves lead to the development of a critical sense; they may even mislead us into supposing we know something about poetry if we can use them correctly. Far better to acquire a critical sense as we read poetry for enjoyment, and pick up the technical terms as we go along.

How then do we acquire a critical sense? Briefly, by reading as much poetry as we can, and by reflecting on what we read. There is no surer way. A handbook of poetical criticism similar to a handbook on motor-car engines would be worse than useless. Motor-car engines are mass-produced; poems are not. Every poem has a life of its own. That is why every poem must be criticized individually.

Every poem has a life of its own. It is a fragment of the life of a poet, which is a part of the life of mankind. A trivial poem is an unimportant fragment; a great poem is an important fragment. *King Lear* is an immense fragment of the poetic life of a man who was an immense part of the life of a great period in the history of a great nation. Even a little poem, provided it is good, is a part of life worth study and reflection. Poetry is as rich and various as life itself; to poets, it *is* life. Poetry is a world, of which poets are the articulate and readers the inarticulate part. If we are to read poetry for its full significance and satisfaction, we must see it against the background of this rich and various poetic world. A poem is not an isolated piece of expression that can be put on a mental mantelpiece like a picture postcard, to be glanced at and forgotten. As a fragment from the poets' world, with a life of its own, however small, it enters into the conscious and subconscious experience of the reader, making it thenceforward richer and, in however slight a degree, different. If the reading of poems is not an enlargement of experience, it is a waste of time. We read a poem with the purpose of trying to discover the essential life within it—in other words, the poet's intention, conscious or unconscious; if the poet's experience is new, it makes an addition to the life of poetry, and so, if we read it truly, to our own lives. If we discover it to be false, second-hand, or shoddy, it has nothing to give us and we reject it. If by attention and care we have, during our reading of poems, allowed and encouraged our critical sense to develop, we shall *feel* the essential nature of any new poem we read and know whether it is of value. For instance, during the 1920's poets and readers of sensibility became aware of the poems of the Jesuit priest Gerard Manley Hopkins, who had died almost unknown thirty years before. It was felt instinctively that these were poems of unique worth. Something in the poems themselves—their originality, urgency and seriousness—compelled attention. Hopkins became the fashion; but now that mere fashion in Hopkins has had its day, most intelligent poets and critics agree in giving Hopkins a very high place in English poetry, and perhaps the highest place of all in Victorian poetry. A developed critical sense, then, a trained poetic taste will be ready to accept what is new for its essential value. We first *feel* a new poem to possess a true and individual life within it; afterwards we reflect on it and analyse it to find out in what its uniqueness consists. We may find we have been mistaken; we can be taken in by dishonest poetry as easily as by a dishonest person. Only experience of poetry, like experience of people, can protect us against the false and specious.

2

I have called poetry a world because only so can I give an impression of its variety, its unity, and its completeness within itself. In one small book no more than a suggestion can be given of its many forms and complexions. In looking at a poem we shall try to see it as a whole; even in examining details we shall try to keep in mind the whole poem, the complete object of which they are only parts. What is the poet trying to say? What is the experience he is trying to communicate? What is the object he is trying to shape out of the unshaped mass of his experience, feelings, and impressions? In what way is it original, unique, valuable? By what means does he achieve or fail to achieve these ends? Content and form, experience and technique, meaning and means— the pattern is a circular one: we could start to examine it at any point. For content determines form and form modifies content. Although it is usually easier and more logical to examine content first, then form, we must keep both in mind simultaneously. In the process of composition the interaction is probably continuous. A poet does not first think what he is going to say and then decide how he is going to say it. Form and content are determined simultaneously. Here we could make a long digression to discuss what we know of various poets' methods of composition. Perhaps we could sum up the discussion in this way: poets have at different times shown varying degrees of preoccupation with form and with content. At the time of Pope, for instance, acceptable poetic forms were very limited; for serious poetry the heroic couplet exercised almost a monopoly. If Pope had something to say, he had hardly to consider the form in which he could say it; he habitually used the heroic couplet. Although, therefore, he was outwardly concerned with style, as his paraphrases of Boileau in *An Essay on Criticism* show, he was interested in form only in a very limited sense. What he did not realize was that the choice of a fixed pattern limited what he might express; for only restricted emotions can be expressed in the heroic couplet. Pope's main concern was with the problem of what to say; and in his case this meant laying down the laws of thought and conduct in polite society.

Fifty years after his death Wordsworth and Coleridge were preoccupied with the problems of form, and Wordsworth had much to say about poetic diction and the fashions set by Pope and his followers. But his preoccupation with form was due, essentially, to the desire to say new things; it sprang from a concern with content. The novel ideas which he had to express in his poems could not be expressed in stereotyped forms.

Concern with form is in reality always a concern with content. New ideas demand new forms. To-day there are almost no accepted forms—or rather, almost any form is acceptable. More than ever before, each poem has to be looked at for its individual essence. If a modern poet chooses the sonnet form, for example, it does not follow that his thought is conservative or that it could have been uttered in just that way in the time of Shakespeare or Wordsworth, both writers of sonnets. In the age of Pope, perhaps, too much was sacrificed to conformity, to-day the lack of conformity, or rather, the absence of any accepted poetic forms, is a stumbling-block to understanding. But it makes it all the more important to give poets our close and unprejudiced attention.

Before undertaking some practical criticism, a further warning must be given. In spite of the efforts of some modern critics to place the criticism of poetry on a scientific basis and establish standards which are independent of private judgement, criticism remains a highly subjective process. Every reader is an individual human being. All his attitudes, especially in aesthetic matters, will be conditioned by his prejudices and predispositions. These are in turn determined by childhood influences and other factors which differ in the case of every single individual. However 'scientifically' and objectively we suppose ourselves to react to a work of art, our minds are for the most part made up for us, even before we look at the object in view, by influences outside ourselves. We go to a picture gallery and immediately admire some picture because it reminds us of someone we love or some place of pleasant memory, or because of some quite unimportant detail which strikes our fancy or arouses our interest. Thereupon we try to justify our preference on critical grounds. I am sure this is done by even the most respected and note worthy art critics. We may like something simply because it is fashionable, or because it has been admired by someone we admire. All this is perfectly legitimate, and indeed inevitable, provided we realize the limitations of our judgement.

All that we can hope for is a consensus of opinion among people of like minds and educated taste. Unfortunately even this can scarcely be expected in poetic appreciation. There are no generally accepted canons of taste in poetry. This is not to say that every critic's judgement is equally sound, or that preference is solely a matter of individual whim and fancy. It does mean, however, that no one—or anyone—can speak with the voice of authority. It means also that a reader must judge for himself among critics. If a critic can make sense of a poem that baffles the reader, if he can show convincing reasons why a poem he has previously liked is good, or not good; if he can reveal something of the life within a poem and illuminate it by his remarks—then he has a right to be heard, and the reader will do well to listen to him.

The best that any critic can do, in the long run, is to show the reader how to develop his own standards, to show him how to make himself independent of fashion in matters of taste. A good critic contrives to be at once assured yet unassertive, he makes his own views clear and unmistakable, but does not try to impose them by overstatement and force of will. He must, indeed, write dogmatically; he will gain no confidence if his standards appear uncertain and wavering. But he can, in the end, do no more than reveal as persuasively and eloquently as possible the things that have moved him most deeply, and leave it to the reader to follow or to dissent, according as his own tastes and predilections prompt. For these reasons Coleridge and Hazlitt and Lamb were better critics than Pope and Dr Johnson.

3

Hard Frost

Frost called to water 'Halt!'
And crusted the moist snow with sparkling salt;
Brooks, their own bridges, stop,
And icicles in long stalactites drop,
And tench in water holes
Lurk under gluey glass like fish in bowls.

In the hard-rutted lane
At every footstep breaks a brittle pane,
And tinkling trees ice-bound,
Changed into weeping willows, sweep the ground;
Dead boughs take root in ponds
And ferns on windows shoot their ghostly fronds.

But vainly the fierce frost
Interns poor fish, ranks trees in an armed host,
Hangs daggers from house-eaves
And on the windows ferny ambush weaves;
In the long war grown warmer
The sun will strike him dead and strip his armour.

ANDREW YOUNG

This poem is no more than an extended and elaborated metaphor. It does not aim at saying much about nature nor at making any profound observation. It is unpretentious, accurate, and witty rather than passionate. The wit lies in the way in which the military metaphor is worked out.

Metaphor is one of the oldest and most fundamental expressions in language of the human imagination. The imagination is one of the ways in which men extend their knowledge of life and extend their consciousness over a larger field than their immediate surroundings. In perceiving imaginatively the possible relations between things apparently unlike, the poet creates new, beautiful, and surprising ideas. The following riddle-poem is said to be more than a thousand years old.

QUOTATION

27

> White bird featherless
> Flew from Paradise,
> Pitched on the castle wall;
> Along came Lord Landless,
> Took it up handless,
> And rode away horseless to the King's white hall.*

This is a charming poem, and its charm is independent of its meaning. The 'white bird' is the snow, and 'Lord Landless' is the sun. The folk imagination, like that of children, delights in riddles, and a metaphor is often no more than a literary form of the riddle.

Andrew Young, a modern nature poet, recaptures something of the primitive simplicity and purity of vision of a child. By discarding sophisticated and moralistic notions about nature—such notions, for instance, as those made current by Wordsworth—he achieves a fresh and original vision. Not that his poems are, in any other sense, 'primitive'; they are civilized, but it is his treatment that is civilized; his vision remains child-like.

Just as the old riddle suggests a conflict between sun and snow, so Young writes of the sun doing battle against, and

---

* This is of course a comparatively modern version. See *The Oxford Dictionary of Nursery Rhymes.*

finally routing, frost. The military metaphor is begun in the opening line:

> Frost called to water 'Halt!'

For a few lines the war seems to be forgotten: brooks build ice bridges, icicles hang in stalactites, fish are frozen in. Brittle panes glaze the cart-ruts, the trees are transformed into weeping willows, and the frost plants ferns on the windows. But all these transformations are part of the war between frost and sun; for the fish are 'interned' like suspects in time of war; the frozen trees are 'an armed host'; the icicles are 'daggers'; the ferns of frost on the window are 'an ambush'. Finally, as the sun grows warmer, it will kill frost 'and strip him of his armour'.

This is perhaps too ingenious to be truly satisfying, perhaps a little artificial. So some will think. But we must not expect too much from a short poem, a poem which makes no claim to greatness or depth. There is, in fact, much more in Young's short, relatively few nature poems than a casual reader will find. If we read them carefully, we shall remember them long after more showy pieces have been forgotten. They are not the whole of poetry, they may indeed be only a small part of it, but they are truly poetic throughout.

Young is not a strikingly original technician, but his versification is always adequate to what he has to say. He is content with slight variations on traditional forms. Here, for instance, he uses with consistent skill a combination of the octosyllabic and the five-foot couplet—the first line having four and the second five feet. There is no obvious reason for this device, dictated no doubt by the writer's instinct, as such things usually are. Perhaps it is fanciful to suggest that the first line in each pair, having only four feet, strikes us as crisp, brittle and cramped, like frost; while the second, the five-foot line, with its freer movement, gives a suggestion of the sense of impending release when the frost shall be thawed. But whatever the cause, the rhythm, the stark, precise diction, and clear imagery seem exactly what the poem requires.

4

The Owl

Downhill I came, hungry, and yet not starved;
Cold, yet had heat within me that was proof
Against the North wind; tired, yet so that rest
Had seemed the sweetest thing under a roof.

Then at the inn I had food, fire, and rest,
Knowing how hungry, cold, and tired was I.
All of the night was quite barred out except
An owl's cry, a most melancholy cry

Shaken out long and clear upon the hill,
No merry note, nor cause of merriment,
But one telling me plain what I escaped
And others could not, that night, as in I went.

And salted was my food, and my repose,
Salted and sobered, too, by the bird's voice
Speaking for all who lay under the stars,
Soldiers and poor, unable to rejoice.

EDWARD THOMAS

This poem expresses a feeling of compassion for poor and unsheltered people on a cold night, a sense of community between a sheltered individual and a mass of unknown people less fortunate than he. Such a theme could easily produce sentimentality; for the commonest source of sentimentality is the feeling of pity for abstract humanity. Sentimentality is one of the commonest human weaknesses, and it would be well to say a little more about it, because it is one of the commonest causes of bad poetry. Sentimentality is emotion gone wrong; though not necessarily insincere, it always has an element of falsity. When we are sentimental, we are getting something for nothing, pretending we feel deeply about something we cannot really feel about at all. It is sentimental to proclaim a sense of grief, for instance, at the woes of people we never saw or knew when we do nothing, and can do nothing, to alleviate their woes. It is mere self-indulgence, a wallowing in false emotion at someone else's expense. If we read of a disaster in the newspaper, the reader of real feeling and sensibility is the one who keeps silence; the self-indulgent sentimentalist is the one who enjoys all the details of the disaster and discusses them in a spirit of gloating disguised as sympathy. But it is not easy to draw the line between sentimentality and true feeling. Is everyone who expresses pity for the misfortunes of the unknown a sentimentalist? The answer, it seems, must be: It depends how it is done. If the event causes real distress, real emotion, the reaction is not sentimental. But if it does this, the expression of emotion is likely to be restrained, even painful.

In this poem Edward Thomas gives no details of the sufferings of the poor, and of soldiers. He says simply that they sleep 'under the stars' and not, like him, in a warm and hospitable inn. Moreover, he is concerned, not to expand in sympathy towards the sufferings of others, but simply to record the feelings aroused in him by the melancholy cry of the owl. He does not exaggerate his distress; he says that his own comfort was 'salted and sobered' by the reflections started in his mind by the owl. His whole treatment of the experience is, in other words, restrained. He writes with the sober under-statement beneath which true feeling lies.

There are four four-line verses written in iambic pentameters, the second and fourth in each verse rhyming. The verse-form is simple and regular. The tone is quiet and conversational, and the diction unaffected and almost bare. There is very little imagery; the owl's cry is the only thing in the poem which is described in any detail.

> ... a most melancholy cry,
> Shaken out long and clear upon the hill.

For the rest, there is a noticeable absence of descriptive adjectives and striking effects of any kind. The word 'salted' is the only metaphor in the poem.

In verse 1, the writer tells how he approaches an inn at night, hungry, cold and tired; and he is careful not to over-state his discomforts. In verses 2 and 3 he tells how he finds relief at the inn, and how the whole night is shut out except for the owl's cry,

> No merry note, nor cause of merriment.

Here he refers to the song in *Love's Labour's Lost*, 'When icicles hang by the wall'. The cry reminds him of all those who are without comfort and shelter in the cold night. In verse 4 he expands the idea of the owl's cry as

> Speaking for all who lay under the stars.

We may guess from the reference to soldiers that the poem was written in war-time; it was, indeed, during the First World War that many of Thomas's poems were written. This poem is thus no vague expression of sympathy for those less privileged than the poet; it is the sincere record of a truly felt and disturbing experience. Its tone is quiet, restrained and yet earnest; it avoids all falseness and exaggeration, and never falls, as it easily might, into sentimentality.

5

QUOTATION
29

The Tables Turned

Up! up! my Friend, and quit your books;
Or surely you'll grow double:
Up! up! my Friend, and clear your looks;
Why all this toil and trouble?

The sun, above the mountain's head,
A freshening lustre mellow
Through all the long green fields has spread,
His first sweet evening yellow.

Books! 'tis a dull and endless strife;
Come, hear the woodland linnet,
How sweet his music! on my life,
There's more of wisdom in it.

And hark! how blithe the throstle sings!
He, too, is no mean preacher:
Come forth into the light of things,
Let Nature be your Teacher.

She has a world of ready wealth,
Our minds and hearts to bless—
Spontaneous wisdom breathed by health,
Truth breathed by cheerfulness.

One impulse from a vernal wood
May teach you more of man,
Of moral evil and of good,
Than all the sages can.

Sweet is the lore which Nature brings;
Our meddling intellect
Mis-shapes the beauteous forms of things:—
We murder to dissect.

Enough of Science and of Art;
Close up those barren leaves;
Come forth, and bring with you a heart
That watches and receives.

WILLIAM WORDSWORTH

In the criticism of Edward Thomas's *The Owl*, it was pointed out that, although this poem was concerned with the hardships of the poor and unfortunate, it was not a didactic poem—that is, one which seeks to point out some philosophical truth in poetic language. Wordsworth's *The Tables Turned* is an almost purely didactic poem. The statements it makes about nature and art are meant to be taken at their face value as general truths about life.

To understand the poem fully, we need to know something of the background of political and aesthetic thought at the time it was written—the last decade of the eighteenth century. There was at this time a revolt against formal education and the influence of books, in favour of a return to the direct perception of nature and what Wordsworth calls elsewhere 'the influence of natural objects'. Wordsworth owed much to the thought of Jean-Jacques Rousseau, and the libertarian ideals which had inspired the French Revolution. He professed at this time a blind and almost mystic belief in the power of nature to educate the mind and edify the soul, unaided by human effort. That he came later to abandon this belief does not affect the ardour with which he held and expressed it in the poems of this period.

Although the poem is a sequel to another called *Expostulation and Reply*, it can stand as complete in itself. In the first and second verses his friend is urged to give up the unprofitable study of books and enjoy the beauty of the evening. In verses 3 and 4 the same idea is repeated with emphasis: books are 'a dull and endless strife'; there is more 'wisdom' in the linnet's song, while the throstle is 'no mean preacher'.

> Come forth into the light of things;
> Let Nature be your Teacher.

We are not told what the linnet's wisdom consists in, nor what the throstle preaches, nor the precise quality of Nature's teaching. But in verse 5 we are told of nature's power to bless us, of the wisdom which comes from health and the truth that comes from cheerfulness.

The concluding three verses are a famous statement of Wordsworth's philosophy. It is difficult to see how 'one impulse from a vernal wood' can teach moral evil and good; but the anti-intellectual meaning of verse 6 is clear—and read against the background of eighteenth-century rationalism, it is a reasonable plea for a return to nature. The trouble is that Wordsworth does not tell us what is 'the lore which Nature brings'. Nor is it easy to see how 'a heart That watches and receives' is really 'enough'. Indeed, Wordsworth himself had found, by the time he wrote the *Ode on the Intimations of Immortality*, that it was not enough.

The statement of Wordsworth's belief is bare and almost without imagery; the form is simple, almost paradoxical. As a rational statement, we can hardly take it seriously; it does not bear examination. On rational grounds, the argument is only too easy to confute; it is, indeed, one of the recurring fallacies of all so-called returns to nature that the human intellect is used to argue against the human intellect. There is thus an inevitable basis of insincerity; Wordsworth would not have been himself if he had had no intellect, and it is vain for him to argue against the use of the intellect. The same fallacy was repeated half a century later by the American Whitman, and in the twentieth century by D. H. Lawrence. Yet the revolt against excessive intellectualism is bound to recur periodically. The ideal example of Wordsworth's theory was not Wordsworth himself, but his contemporary John Clare, of whom he knew nothing. Yet Clare did not argue against the intellect, he simply wrote the kind of poetry that could be written by a man in love with nature who brought with him the 'heart that watches and receives'. There is in Clare's poems much more pure observation of nature, much less of the 'meddling intellect' than in Wordsworth's. With Wordsworth, the observation of nature was usually conscious, willed; with Clare it was spontaneous and instinctive. Nevertheless, it should be remembered that Wordsworth's theory and practice had a profound and widespread influence on the poetry of his own day and of succeeding times; Clare himself was a constant admirer of Wordsworth's work. The following is a descriptive poem by Clare.

QUOTATION

30

Signs of Winter

The cat runs races with her tail. The dog
Leaps o'er the orchard hedge and knarls the grass.
The swine run round and grunt and play with straw,
Snatching out hasty mouthfuls from the stack.

Sudden upon the elm-tree tops the crow
Unceremonious visit pays and croaks,
Then swops away. From mossy barns the owl
Bobs hasty out—wheels round and, scared as soon,
As hastily retires. The ducks grow wild
And from the muddy pond fly up and wheel
A circle round the village and soon, tired,
Plunge in the pond again. The maids in haste
Snatch from the orchard hedge the mizzled* clothes
And laughing hurry in to keep them dry.

JOHN CLARE

* misted over.

6

QUOTATION
31

312

may my heart always be open to little
birds who are the secrets of living
whatever they sing is better than to know
and if men should not hear them men are old

may my mind stroll about hungry
and fearless and thirsty and supple
and even if it's sunday may i be wrong
for whenever men are right they are not young

and may myself do nothing usefully
and love yourself so more than truly
there's never been quite such a fool who could fail
pulling all the sky over him with one smile

E. E. CUMMINGS

E. E. Cummings is one of the most individual and original
of modern American poets; but like all truly original poets he

is also truly traditional. The superficial reader is more likely to be struck by the superficial oddity of his poems than by their extreme precision and reasonableness. It is not because they are more difficult, complicated or obscure than much of the poetry we are used to that some readers still find him odd, but because he is in fact simpler. True simplicity is always hard to understand at first. When Wordsworth's simplest poems first appeared they were thought by the official critics of literature to be odd, difficult, and obscure. It was left—as with Cummings—to the poets to discover his true simplicity.

To most superficial readers Cummings is at first irritating. This is a good sign, for it means that something of his originality has got beneath the skin of custom that has grown over the reader's mind. Why no capital letters? he asks. Why not even make that gesture to convention which a capital I for the first person singular would involve? But Cummings makes no gestures to convention. His words mean not only precisely what they mean, their typographical appearance is also part of their meaning. His poems are composed with fastidious and meticulous regard for the precise significance of every word. He does not even give his poems titles, he numbers them. Having deliberately discarded grammatical and typographical conventions, Cummings can record his experience with absolute freshness of impression, strip language of its accidental associations, and reduce it to its barest possible meaning, no more and no less. This is not to say that he is an irresponsible Humpty Dumpty, making words mean what *he* wants. On the contrary, in his poems words mean exactly what they mean and not what the reader may want them to mean. The art of E. E. Cummings is of course highly self-conscious and sophisticated; but his feelings are as spontaneous and natural as can be the feelings of a man living in the highly sophisticated and unnatural atmosphere of modern American urban life. That he is critical of urban America, and frequently satirical about it, is inevitable; yet in the main he accepts it as his natural background, he does not condemn it or retreat from it. He is happy to be alive, to be a man, to have emotions and appetites and thoughts— even in twentieth-century New York.

Yet, sophisticated as he is, intelligent as he is, he mistrusts an excess of sophistication and intelligence. In poem *312* he expresses ideas similar to those of Wordsworth in *The Tables Turned*. Compare with Wordsworth's statements about the linnet and the throstle Cummings'

> birds who are the secrets of living
> whatever they sing is better than to know

Compare with Wordsworth's 'meddling intellect' Cummings'

> and even if it's sunday may i be wrong
> for whenever men are right they are not young

Nevertheless, Cummings' poem is not, like Wordsworth's, didactic. Cummings makes no pretence at expressing more than what he feels at the moment; he is concerned with expressing his personal feelings, he does not advance revolutionary theories about morality and nature. The poem is, in fact, a love poem; and what he says is that he cannot be truly and spontaneously in love unless his impulse can have free and untrammelled expression without the interference of intellect and convention.

Here is a further example by E. E. Cummings, of extreme simplicity of thought and neatness of form. It is at first sight no more than a picture of American boys and girls, generalized as 'eddieandbill' and 'bettyandisbel', leaving their games in the wet spring countryside to follow the faint and distant whistle of the old balloon-seller. The season is 'Just-spring', and the world is 'mud-luscious' and 'puddle-wonderful'. Cummings reacts with child-like pleasure to the healthy attractions of mud and puddles.

QUOTATION

3²

30

in Just-
spring   when the world is mud-
luscious the little
lame balloonman

whistles   far   and wee

and eddieandbill come
running from marbles and
piracies and it's
spring

when the world is puddle-wonderful

the queer
old balloonman whistles
far   and   wee
and bettyandisbel come dancing

from hop-scotch and jump-rope and

it's
spring
and
     the

          goat-footed

balloonMan   whistles
far
and
wee   E. E. CUMMINGS

But there is more in the poem than just a picture. For the balloonman, first lame, becomes towards the end 'goatfooted'. In other words, he is identified with the god Pan—that is why the 'Man' of the last 'balloonMan' suddenly acquires a capital letter. Pan is the God of spring, youth and nature. It is this God whom Cummings' poetic imagination sees—or rather hears—in modern America, and whom boys and girls leave their play to follow, as they did in Greek mythology. Why Just-spring should have a capital letter is not so easily explained; it may be that Cummings wishes to suggest that the season, like the God, is magical. The reader who complains that the poem is set out in an unnecessarily odd way should try setting it out in a more conventional way, to see if the effect is exactly the same.

7

QUOTATION

33

Piazza Piece

—I am a gentleman in a dustcoat trying
To make you hear. Your ears are soft and small
And listen to an old man not at all,
They want the young men's whispering and sighing.
But see the roses on your trellis dying
And hear the spectral singing of the moon;
For I must have my lovely lady soon,
I am a gentleman in a dustcoat trying.

—I am a lady young in beauty waiting
Until my true love comes, and then we kiss.
But what grey man among the vines is this
Whose words are dry and faint as in a dream?
Back from my trellis, Sir, before I scream!
I am a lady young in beauty waiting.

JOHN CROWE RANSOM

John Crowe Ransom is an American poet born in 1888. Like Cummings, his junior by six years, he is a fastidious technician. But whereas Cummings' style is loose, free and experimental, Ransom's is severely traditional. He rarely departs from the five-foot iambic line and the four-line stanza. In *Piazza Piece* he uses the sonnet form, but this is unusual for him. It is in his diction and the internal movement of his lines that his individuality lies.

The structure of *Piazza Piece* is as formal, and at the same time as inevitable, as a minuet by Haydn. The octave begins and ends with the same line; so does the sestet. The poem is obviously in dialogue form, the speaker of the octave being the old gentleman, the speaker of the sestet being the young lady. The formality of the poem is achieved without any sense of strain, and the reader feels that added sense of pleasure which always arises from the contemplation of a skilful, yet natural, formal pattern.

At first reading, the poem seems to do no more than relate an attempt by an old courtier in the artificial setting of an Italian square to get the attention of a young lady, and the lady's decided rejection of his advances. Then a doubt is felt: why is the old gentleman in a 'dustcoat'? Why the dying roses and the ghostly voice of the moon? Roses are the symbol of youthful passion, the moon is a symbol of virginity and death. The dustcoat in this context inevitably suggests 'dusty death'. So we realize that the gentleman is not simply an old gallant, but Death. The poem is a variation on the familiar theme of 'Death and the Maiden'. Ransom invests this classic theme with new beauty and music. The sound-qualities of the words hardly need to be dwelt on. If the poem is spoken aloud, smoothly and not too fast, its music is heard unmistakably. Yet this slow and grave music is achieved without the use of strange or exotic words. The most unusual words in the poem are 'trellis' and 'spectral'—after them there is nothing more odd than 'dustcoat' and 'vines'. Nor is there any oddity of construction: the placing of 'not at all' in the third line has just that faint suggestion of pedantry we might expect from an old courtier. There is, too, a slightly antique flavour in the lady's phrase 'Back from my trellis'. Otherwise, there is nothing odd, not a word out of its normal speech order. The extreme simplicity of the language gives the poem true pathos, the slightly exotic and antique setting give an air of mystery. The thought of the poem is not new, but there are few poems in English of greater formal perfection and power to enchant.

Mention has been made of the 'music' of words, and it is here that a warning should be given. Properly speaking, music is the deliberate arrangement of notes of varying pitch, whether singly or in combination, in a rhythmical pattern or sequence. The purest forms of music are probably instrumental, though of course vocal music includes the sound-qualities of words. It is the fact that words have a sound-quality, as distinct from their sense, that has given rise to the phrase 'the music of words'. This has led some to experiment with word-music and try to invent a poetry which is independent of sense. Such experiments are bound to be abortive, because we cannot detach the sound of a word from its sense. Words in combination have rhythm, and certain words are smoother of utterance than others; indeed, most poetry is to some extent onomatopoeic. We can rightly speak of the 'music' of:

> All the birds of the air fell a-sighing and a-sobbing,
>   When they heard of the death of poor Cock Robin,

of the lines

>   Nymphs and shepherds, come away

and

> Over the hills and far away,

or

> Full fathom five thy father lies,
> Of his bones are coral made;
> Those are pearls that were his eyes.

But the sense of the lines is of much greater importance in arousing emotion than the sound. It is, I believe, almost impossible to attend closely to the sound of words and ignore their sense. True, we can listen to poetry read in a language we do not understand, and feel that Dante, for instance, is more musical than most German poets; we can observe that Anglo-Saxon poetry sounds harsher than French. But we should soon grow weary of listening to any language, however beautiful, for its sound alone; moreover, we should have little notion of the real value and beauty of the poetry. The most trivial popular rhyme in Italian might sound better than a speech from Goethe's *Faust*.

Yet the sound-qualities of language are important, and all good poets have been aware of them; no poet of the first rank strikes us as having had a poor ear. The language of Tennyson is mellifluous to the point of excess; the language of Donne is sometimes harsh, but deliberately so. Donne's 'music' is part of the man, and is the result of his temperamental impatience with the sugared notes of much of the love poetry of his time. We cannot call him unmusical; we can only say that his music was very different from Spenser's.

When we speak of the music of poetry, we should remember that it is necessarily a much less important and determining constituent than meaning. At its best, as in the sonnet by John Crowe Ransom, it is so bound up with the meaning that we can hardly think of it as existing separately. The same is true of *Kubla Khan*, which has long been considered one of the most musical poems in English. But the music is never felt to have been applied, apart from the sense, as we often feel in Tennyson. Coleridge had an unusually sensitive poetic ear; we cannot say this about Wordsworth; nobody reads Wordsworth for the sound alone, though many have so read *Kubla Khan*. Some, indeed, have mistakenly found it beautiful nonsense. It is not nonsense; it is indeed a profound reflection on the nature of poetry and on Coleridge's personal tragedy. Not a word in it is chosen for its sound alone; nor yet for its meaning alone. Both functions of language are simultaneously given due importance by what we can only regard as a miraculous instinct for selection. Usually in poetry, either we can say easily whether a word has been chosen mainly for its sound or its sense; or, as is more common, since words are for the most part chosen mainly for sense, we feel that the sound-qualities of the poem are inferior to the sense. In *Kubla Khan* the fusion is perfect, the choice is unerring. Shakespeare, and sometimes Blake, have this capacity also, more than most other poets. Most poets do not satisfy the ear simultaneously with the mind and feelings very often. The best poetry does so, and does it in such a way as to make us unaware of any separation of ear and mind. The poem isolates itself, so to speak, from its context in ordinary experience to take on a separate, unique and indestructible existence of its own—independent not only of our ordinary experience, but also of its own separate constituents of sense and sound. Such are the best sonnets of Shakespeare and the best lyrics of Blake. Some of Hamlet's soliloquies have also this quality, which can only be called a sort of intellectual music.

8

Ozymandias

I met a traveller from an antique land
Who said: Two vast and trunkless legs of stone
Stand in the desert.... Near them, on the sand,
Half sunk, a shattered visage lies, whose frown,
And wrinkled lip, and sneer of cold command,
Tell that its sculptor well those passions read
Which yet survive, stamped on these lifeless things,
The hand that mocked them, and the heart that fed:
And on the pedestal these words appear:
'My name is Ozymandias, king of kings:
Look on my works, ye Mighty, and despair!'
Nothing beside remains. Round the decay
Of that colossal wreck, boundless and bare
The lone and level sands stretch far away.

P. B. SHELLEY

In considering the sonnet *Piazza Piece* by John Crowe
Ransom, we noted its formal perfection. The sonnet is
perhaps the most difficult form in English poetry in which to
achieve perfection. It is a very strict form: the thought has
to be made to fit into fourteen iambic pentameters, no more and
no less, having one of several possible rhyme-schemes. If
the thought overflows the mould, there may be an effect of
excessive compression; on the other hand, if the poet has not
quite enough to say, there will be padding. The Victorian
priest Gerard Manley Hopkins wrote sonnets with great
compression of thought, as did the Jacobean priest John
Donne. On the other hand, it is a satisfying form for a poet
of reasonable skill. It is of a length not to discourage learning

by heart; it allows of the adequate expansion of a single thought, but is too short to allow of digression and repetition. Its popularity among poets of nearly every generation since the middle of the sixteenth century, when it was introduced, is due to these factors, and to its being a fairly hard test of skill. English poetry has on the whole avoided rigid formalism and external rules; it may be that poets have turned with relief to a form which imposes strict limits to thought and expression.

Shelley was temperamentally opposed to external discipline, and this may be why he did not excel, as some of his contemporaries did, in the sonnet form. *Ozymandias* is his only well-known sonnet; although the thought is clear and striking, the poem is not, from the formal point of view, completely successful.

The first line puts the experience in a remote setting: this is a traveller's tale, and this relieves Shelley of any need for historical accuracy. The scene is probably Egypt or North Africa. One of the hereditary titles of the Kings of Ethiopia is 'King of Kings'. The phrase 'vast and trunkless' does not perfectly apply to legs; 'vast' means 'of great extent', and the legs would be tall rather than vast. After 'in the desert' the phrase 'in the sand' is hardly necessary. 'Visage' means 'face'. If the face is 'shattered'—that is, broken to pieces—it would be difficult to recognize its 'frown, and wrinkled lip, and sneer', especially if it was 'half sunk'. A further logical difficulty arises: these marks of expression on the face of the statue tell us that the sculptor could well read the passions fed by the tyrant's heart. This is to assume that he was a good sculptor, for we know nothing more of him or of his subject. He might have been a bad sculptor and mis-read his master's heart; for there is nothing in a portrait to tell us whether it is a good likeness unless we know from another source what the subject looked like. But it may be that the legend on the pedestal suggests a cold-hearted tyrant. In this case, the word before 'on the pedestal these words appear' should be 'for', not 'and'.

'The decay of that colossal wreck' is tautological. Even if stone can be said to 'decay', it is hardly necessary to speak of the decay of a 'wreck'. But Shelley was under the necessity of completing his iambic pentameter with an 'ay' rhyme. 'Boundless and bare, the lone and level sands stretch far away' is similarly repetitive: 'bare' and 'lone' are hardly both necessary; and if the sands are 'boundless', it need not be added that they stretch 'far away'. But the attractions of the alliteration in 'boundless and bare' and 'lone and level' are perhaps intended to compensate for the thinness of the imaginative detail. Word-music has here taken precedence over sense.

This is not a bad poem. The double meaning in 'Look on my works, ye Mighty, and despair' has an irony which was worth pointing out; the statement of the futility of despotism was in keeping with Shelley's thought and the libertarian ideas of his time. But it is not a good sonnet, and it is clear that Shelley was not at ease in this form; nor does the poem bear the marks of personal experience.

9

QUOTATION

35

The Expiration

So, so, breake off this last lamenting kisse,
　　Which sucks two soules, and vapors Both away,
Turne thou ghost that way, and let mee turne this,
　　And let our selves benight our happiest day,
We ask'd none leave to love; nor will we owe
　　Any, so cheape a death, as saying, Goe;

> Goe; and if that word have not quite kil'd thee,
>   Ease mee with death, by bidding mee goe too.
> Oh, if it have, let my word worke on mee,
>   And a just office on a murderer doe.
> Except it be too late, to kill me so,
>   Being double dead, going and bidding, goe.
>   JOHN DONNE

Donne was unexcelled in expressing the pain of separation in love. 'Let us,' he says here, 'break off our final kiss. Like two ghosts let us go our separate ways; let us deliberately, without help from others, turn our happiest day into night. Go: and if the word has not killed you, kill me by telling me to go. If you are already dead, let my command to go avenge your murder by killing me—unless, that is, I am already doubly dead from the pain of leaving you and telling you to go.'

Perhaps the argument is forced and intellectual. But if we have read Donne's other love poems, we shall recognize here that contorted and despairing rationalization which anguish always causes him. It is as if, in moments of extreme emotion, his brain was more than ordinarily active, so that the argument overflows the emotion and goes a little beyond reason to the verge of the ridiculous. To Donne, passionate to the point of hysteria, hyperbole was a natural habit of expression. Again and again he represents the pain of separation as death; to others it may at the time seem *like* death; to Donne it is death itself.

But the force and compulsion of this poem lie, not in any literal statement, nor in reasoned argument, but in the language and rhythm. It is impossible to read it aloud, or even to the inward ear, without being aware of its passion and sincerity, despite the near absurdity of the meaning. It is worth while, therefore, looking more closely at its technical features. Let us try to discover how it achieves its compelling power.

In discussing Ransom's *Piazza Piece*, we spoke of its formal symmetry and its word-music. Here we have a somewhat similar structure. The first verse begins 'So, so'; and ends 'Goe'. The second verse begins with the word 'Goe' and ends with the same word. This symmetry is achieved without the slightest strain. Despite the immense force of the emotion, the poem has been compressed between rigid formal limits. It is the 'Goe' at the beginning of verse 2 which is the centre and pivot of the poem: in the first verse he has been bracing himself to utter the word of finality; and this is the word; he has uttered it. The situation has therefore the dramatic power of actuality; Donne is not writing *about* an experience; the poem itself *is* the experience in all its immediacy and finality.

The very sound and rhythm of the words are part of the experience; they have the grave urgency of the march of doom; the rhythm is regular without being smooth. This must be due in part to the preponderance of monosyllables. In verse 1 the only words of more than one syllable are: lamenting, vapours, benight, happiest (all important words), away, any and saying, which are scarcely more than monosyllables. Moreover, not a word is out of its natural prose order, and the rhymes are therefore quite unforced. Such writing is a triumph—whether of skill or instinct it does not matter. The sense of inevitability is overwhelming.

In verse 2 there are eight disyllables (murderer is scanned as a disyllable), but four of them are words ending in -ing and hardly affect the generally monosyllabic character of the lines. Only one line, the fourth, contains an inversion of the prose order. Although the second verse appears a little more contrived than the first, the poem as a whole is marvellously direct and natural. Milton said that poetry should be 'simple, sensuous, and passionate'; Wordsworth called it 'the spontaneous overflow of powerful feeling'. Neither was thinking of Donne when he wrote; yet these descriptions apply almost exactly to this poem. 'Sensuous' is the only word of doubtful application; it is true that the main force of the poem seems to come from its compact lines of monosyllables with little emotional colour.

> Turne thou ghost that way, and let mee turne this

and

> Goe, and if that word have not quite kil'd thee;

yet there are sufficient words of sensuous appeal to lend to the expression the feeling of concreteness and actuality: lamenting kisse, sucks, ghost, murderer.

But whatever analytical care we exercise, we cannot say finally, 'This is what Donne felt—and this is how he expressed it.' Experience and expression, content and form, emotion and diction—each seems to grow out of the other, to be part of it, and indistinguishable.

QUOTATION
36

The Computation

For the first twenty yeares, since yesterday
  I scarce beleev'd, thou could'st be gone away,
For forty more, I fed on favours past,
  And forty' on hopes, that thou would'st, they might last.
Teares drown'd one hundred, and sighes blew out two,
  A thousand, I did neither thinke nor doe,
  Or not divide, all being one thought of you;
  Or in a thousand more, forgot that too.
Yet call not this long life; But thinke that I
Am, by being dead, Immortall; Can ghosts die?

JOHN DONNE

Here the same thought, the pain of parting, is expressed in terms of extreme hyperbole; some readers may consider it merely witty, and indeed it has less emotional force than *The Expiration*. What Donne seeks to do is to convey a sense of the extremity of his suffering; rationally considered, his argument is ludicrous, but as an emotional statement it is perfectly reasonable.

> For the first twenty years, since yesterday
> I scarce believ'd, thou could'st be gone away,

Only in this exaggerated way can he express the sense of stunned incomprehension which separation has produced. He then goes through the various states of mind which have succeeded, allotting to each a fantastic period of time—forty years for thinking on his mistress's past favours, another forty on hopes of future favours, a hundred for tears, two hundred for sighs, and so on. He concludes by saying that the total of all these years does not mean he has lived a long life; no, the separation killed him, and he has become immortal. He is now only the ghost of his former self; will death once more put an end to his sufferings?

This is a witty poem, but it is at the same time passionate; it is intellectual, but prompted by intense feeling. This is one of the rarest combinations found in English poetry, and one found more often in Donne than in any other poet. It is a characteristic of the later Renaissance, one carried over from the Elizabethan period into the seventeenth century, when it became one of the central features of the school of poets known as the Metaphysicals. After the seventeenth century, we find the eighteenth mistrusting passion and the nineteenth mistrusting reason; so that there was for long a divorce between the two. It was not until the twentieth century that wit and passion are once more found combined

in poetry—unless we except the solitary figure of Gerard
Manley Hopkins, in whose best poems religious fervour is
found wedded to intellectual energy, and neither allowed to
dominate.

10

QUOTATION

37

God's Grandeur

The world is charged with the grandeur of God.
　It will flame out, like shining from shook foil;
　It gathers to a greatness, like the ooze of oil
Crushed. Why do men then now not reck his rod?
Generations have trod, have trod, have trod;
　And all is seared with trade; bleared, smeared with toil;
　And wears man's smudge and shares man's smell: the soil
Is bare now, nor can foot feel, being shod.

And for all this, nature is never spent;
　There lives the dearest freshness deep down things;
And though the last lights off the black West went
　Oh, morning, at the brown brink eastward, springs—
Because the Holy Ghost over the bent
　World broods with warm breast and with ah! bright wings
　　　　　　　　　　　　　GERARD MANLEY HOPKINS

Only in its rhyme-scheme is this sonnet traditional in form
Both in its rhythm and in its sentence structure it is highly
original. Hopkins was so original that his poems were no
fully appreciated until nearly forty years after his death. I
is difficult to realize that this sonnet was written in 1877
Hopkins foreshadowed modern developments in poetry in a
truly prophetic manner. In one respect above all he was a
poet of the twentieth, not the nineteenth century. His poem
are written to be read with precision, every word is importan

for what it actually says, not for vague poetic association and suggestiveness. He broke away from the romantic tradition of Keats and Shelley which was carried on through Victorian times in the poems of Tennyson and Swinburne. As a poet he looks back to the seventeenth century and is spiritually akin more to the later Donne than to religious poets of his own time such as Christina Rossetti and Francis Thompson.

In the first three lines (including the next word, 'crushed') of *God's Grandeur* he uses two images to describe his subject: God's grandeur shines out from the world like the gleam from shaken foil, presumably tin or lead foil—he may here have been thinking of some electrical experiment, which would explain the word 'charged' in line 1; and there is an earlier version of the poem in which 'lightning' is used in line 2 instead of 'shining'; it is also like the gradual accumulation of oil in a vat when olives are crushed. Thus the two characteristics of God's grandeur which Hopkins wishes to stress are its flashing brightness and its secret, slow richness.

The next passage is not easy to paraphrase. What Hopkins is saying is that men take no heed of God's punishments—everything is soiled with the stains of labour and striving; the whole earth, which ought to shine with the grandeur of God, is made foul with the marks of man's toil. The earth is worn bare by men's toiling feet, which cannot feel it through their shoes.

Yet, he goes on, in spite of the effects of industry and trade, nature is not exhausted; deep down, a precious natural freshness remains. Even though utter blackness should overcome the world, yet morning waits in the east, as a sign that God broods over it in love and protection.

This is a difficult poem because in attempting to state his meaning with absolute precision Hopkins uses uncommon and unfamiliar imagery. It is not fully successful because the meaning has perhaps been unduly compressed within the limits of the sonnet form. But its compressed meaning can be made to expand under a searching examination. The originality and strangeness of the sentence-structure compels close attention. Hopkins rarely, if ever, wrote for the casual and superficial reader. Yet some of his effects are obvious and bold—for instance, the threefold repetition of 'have trod' in line 5 gives an overwhelming sense of ceaseless and monotonous effort. It seems, too, as if in the final phrase, 'warm breast and . . . bright wings', there is a return to the idea of the first two images, that of 'shining from shook foil' and that of the warmth and richness of oil.

I cannot claim to be quite certain of Hopkins' exact intention throughout; and I have deliberately chosen for discussion a poem containing some ambiguities. Other readers may see an intention which has escaped my analysis. For instance, I am not certain that the 'foil' in line 2 is metallic foil, which is a product of industry and therefore might not be suitable in this context. Hopkins may have in mind simply the original meaning of the word—'leaf'. In this case the two images, 'leaf' and 'crushed oil', refer to springtime and harvest. This possibility is strengthened by the fact that the leaves of the olive-tree shine, almost sparkle, when shaken by the wind.

II

The three sonnets so far discussed, by John Crowe Ransom, Shelley, and Hopkins, are all of the Miltonic or Petrarcan type. This type is divided into two more or less clearly separated parts—the octave (first 8 lines) and the sestet (last 6 lines). In the octave a single argument or thought is stated and developed; in the sestet the argument is concluded; often the sestet presents a contrasting point of view to that developed in the octet.

This, however, is not the only type of the sonnet in English. The other is usually known as the Shakespearean, from the fact that Shakespeare was its greatest exponent. He was, indeed, probably the only poet of the first rank to use this form of the sonnet. It consists, not of an octave and a sestet, but of three quatrains (4-line verses) followed by a rhymed couplet (2 lines). The great disadvantage of the form is obvious: too much emphasis is inclined to fall on the final couplet, which often assumes the appearance of a sententious tag affixed at the end. Its two lines do not give enough room to develop a thought or an argument fully. Shakespeare himself does not always overcome this difficulty satisfactorily; but in his best sonnets he triumphs, as in other forms, over the difficulties of the medium.

QUOTATION

38

> Since brass, nor stone, nor earth, nor boundless sea,
> But sad mortality o'ersways their power,
> How with this rage shall beauty hold a plea
> Whose action is no stronger than a flower?
> O, how shall summer's honey breath hold out
> Against the wreckful siege of battering days,
> When rocks impregnable are not so stout,
> Nor gates of steel so strong, but Time decays?
> O fearful meditation! where, alack,
> Shall Time's best jewel from Time's chest lie hid?
> Or what strong hand can hold his swift foot back?
> Or who his spoil of beauty can forbid?
> O, none, unless this miracle have might,
> That in black ink my love may still shine bright.
>
> WILLIAM SHAKESPEARE

Here he is writing on a theme which occupies many of his sonnets—the cruelty of Time. His love will inevitably be devoured by the ravages of time, and the only hope of securing immortality is through his, Shakespeare's, verses.

'Since (he says in the first quatrain) there is no object however durable it appears, immune from "sad mortality" how can my love's beauty escape destruction, being so much more frail?' In the second quatrain he repeats this idea in a different form: Time is a besieger against whose battering rams the sweet breath of summer cannot hope to hold out.

'O fearful meditation!' he cries, at the beginning of the third quatrain. 'How can my love's beauty ("Time's best jewel") be kept from the grave? Is there no power which can stay the swift ravages of Time?'

The only hope, he concludes, lies in the miraculous preservation of his love's memory through the immortality of his verse.

The poem is rhetorical in style. It consists of a series of five questions, all expanding a single idea, and all resolved in the final couplet. It is the sonnet of a dramatist, accustomed to writing for oral declamation. Its full force cannot be felt until it is read aloud. It is then that we realize how much of its force comes from the variation and subtlety of the rhythm. It begins in a tone of measured solemnity, and continues in this way until the seventh line, when a new rhythmical figure appears:

> When rocks impregnable are not so stout,
> Nor gates of steel so strong, but Time decays.

The triple hammer blows of 'rocks impreg-', and 'not so stout', and 'steel so strong', are like the blows of time's battering-ram. The same figure appears twice in the eleventh line:

> Or *what strong hand* can hold his *swift foot back*.

The imagery of the poem stresses the contrast between the

extreme frailty and evanescence of beauty, which is flower-like and soft as breath, and the ruthless strength of time, against which even brass, stone and steel are powerless.

This is a rhetorical poem, and it is also formal, a variation on an often repeated theme; it is a love poem, but it is not at all particularized; the emotion behind it, though we cannot doubt of its strength and sincerity, even of its passion, is generalized. Nothing whatever of the casual or accidental features of the poet's situation is allowed to appear. The writer, or speaker, might, in a sense, be *any* lover oppressed by the sense of 'sad mortality' when contemplating his love's beauty.

For contrast, let us consider a modern love poem, entirely different in spirit and execution.

QUOTATION
39

Meeting at Night

I

The grey sea and the long black land;
And the yellow half-moon large and low;
And the startled little waves that leap
In fiery ringlets from their sleep,
As I gain the cove with pushing prow
And quench its speed i' the slushy sand.

II

Then a mile of warm sea-scented beach;
Three fields to cross till a farm appears;
A tap at the pane, the quick sharp scratch
And blue spurt of a lighted match,
And a voice less loud, thro' its joys and fears,
Than the two hearts beating each to each!

ROBERT BROWNING

Browning wrote this poem about 250 years after Shakespeare's time and 100 years before our own. It consists of two six-line stanzas, each rhyming *abccba*. The metre is four-foot iambic, but is free and irregular owing to the introduction of an anapaest in nearly every line, and the frequent use of spondees. Examples of anapaests are: *as I gain*, *then a mile*, and *and a voice*. Examples of spondees are: *grey sea* and *blue spurt*. This metrical freedom suggests an informal approach to the subject quite unlike that of Shakespeare's sonnet: the tone is at once more conversational and more intimate.

An even greater contrast is presented in the subject-matter of the two poems. Shakespeare is reflecting upon the cruelty of time and the frailty of human beauty; he calls the first part of his sonnet a 'fearful meditation'. Browning does not reflect or meditate at all; he records. What he records is the arrival of a lover (identified with the poet) at evening at a farm near the seashore, where his mistress is waiting for him in darkness; she lights a match as the signal that his tap on the window has been heard (or in order to give light by which she can open the door), and in a moment the two are in each other's arms.

We are told no more; 'joys and fears' are mentioned, and although we can make a general guess as to their nature, we are told nothing precise about them. Yet this brief, poetic record of a meeting between lovers is the reverse of bald or matter-of-fact. It is full of rapture and excitement. These feelings are conveyed, not by direct statement, but partly through the somewhat hurrying rhythm, partly through the diction. There is 'the yellow half-moon large and low'; the leaping wavelets in which the moon is reflected like flames; the 'pushing prow' of the boat whose speed is 'quenched' in the sand; then the 'warm sea-scented beach'. All these suggestions convey the romantic atmosphere of the incident without lingering on it. To linger at all would be to lose the feeling of breathless secrecy which prepares us for the final succession of events—the tap at the farm window, the lighted match, the lovers' whispered greetings.

To recapture the excitement of such an incident in all its immediacy, without over-statement or sentimentality, needed skill and tact: skill in choosing exactly the right words to convey each successive impression, and tact in keeping the movement of the poem free and light. The poem keeps its air of spontaneity after a hundred years, and this must have demanded a considerable poetic gift. There is only one device which 'dates' the poem—the abbreviation in *i' the* and *thro'*. In other respects it is surprisingly 'modern'. It should be compared also with Wordsworth's 'Strange fits of passion I have known' (p. 134).

12

A number of references have been made to imagery in poetry. A full discussion of this subject would take us far beyond the limits of the present book; by nothing can a poet be recognized more surely than by his imagery. The pictures, objects, sounds, even the tastes, textures and smells which continually recur in a poet's work are one of the marks of his individuality. Richness and variety of imagery may be a sign that a poet is more than usually sensitive to physical impressions; thinness or bareness of imagery is not necessarily a sign of imaginative poverty: it may simply be that in this case thought and reflection are more absorbing than physical sensation.

A capacity for vivid sensuous suggestion has always been regarded as one of the most remarkable characteristics of the poetry of Keats. Some critics have praised him for this; others have censured him for indulging it to excess; none has doubted its influence in all his writing, from the earliest to the latest. His exclamation 'O for a life of sensations rather than of thoughts!' at which moralists used to shake their heads, means little more than that the life of sensation had always brought him joy, while thought could not but be painful, since the material circumstances of his life were full of anxiety and distress. He was no shallow sensationalist; strenuous intellectual effort was part of his being, however much unhappiness it caused him. Yet his poems abound in evidence of his appetite for sensation, and are, as we should expect, loaded, some would say overloaded, with sensuous imagery.

We shall in this section examine the imagery of the ode *To Autumn*, one of his best poems; but first, it may be worth while to look at three short and simple examples from other poems. The first two are pictures from *I stood tip-toe upon a little hill*, which he wrote when he was twenty-one.

QUOTATION
40

Here are sweet peas, on tip-toe for a flight:
With wings of gentle flush o'er delicate white,
And taper fingers catching at all things,
To bind them all about with tiny rings. . . .

. . . Where swarms of minnows show their little heads,
Staying their wavy bodies 'gainst the streams,
To taste the luxury of sunny beams
Temper'd with coolness. How they ever wrestle
With their own sweet delight, and ever nestle
Their silver bellies on the pebbly sand.
If you but scantily hold out the hand,
That very instant not one will remain;
But turn your eye, and they are there again.

JOHN KEATS

These are both examples of visual imagery—imagery, that is, which appeals mainly to the eye; both have the power to call up in the reader's mind similar pictures from his own experience. They are fresh, natural, and immediate.

Such a gift for natural description does not in itself constitute poetic greatness; yet it is just the absence of this gift in much of the writing of lesser poets which makes it dull and insipid. Keats's writing is sometimes bad, sometimes trivial, but rarely flat or colourless; it is nearly always alive.

Let us look next at the well-known last verse of *A Song about Myself*, which Keats sent to his young sister Fanny in a letter written from Scotland when he was twenty-three.

QUOTATION
41

There was a naughty boy,
    And a naughty boy was he
He ran away to Scotland
    The people for to see—
        There he found
        That the ground
        Was as hard,
        That a yard
        Was as long,
        That a song
        Was as merry,
        That a cherry
        Was as red—
        That lead
        Was as weighty,
        That fourscore
        Was as eighty,
        That a door
        Was as wooden
        As in England—

So he stood in his shoes
And he wonder'd,
He wonder'd,
He stood in his shoes
And he wonder'd.

JOHN KEATS

Some would call this mere doggerel; it was not intended to be more than a trifle to amuse his sister. He himself said he was ashamed of 'such stuff', written when he was tired after a long day's tramping. Mr. Middleton Murry suggests that it may even have been composed in his head while tramping the hard Scotch miles, and that its rhythm echoes this movement. It is quoted here to show how readily Keats conveys physical sensation, not only visual but also appealing to the ear, the taste, and the touch, even in verses of which he was ashamed. He makes us feel the hard ground and the weight of lead, hear the merry song, see and taste the red cherry. These lines have the neatness, spontaneity, physical solidity, and economy of language of a good nursery rhyme; they are the utterance of a natural poet.

It was the same poet who, little more than a year later, wrote his great ode *To Autumn*, in which so much actual sensation is recaptured in the imagery, but in which there is much more than mere sensation.

QUOTATION

42

To Autumn

Season of mists and mellow fruitfulness,
    Close bosom-friend of the maturing sun;
Conspiring with him how to load and bless
    With fruit the vines that round the thatch-eaves run;

To bend with apples the moss'd cottage-trees,
   And fill all fruit with ripeness to the core;
     To swell the gourd, and plump the hazel shells
   With a sweet kernel; to set budding more,
And still more, later flowers for the bees,
Until they think warm days will never cease,
     For Summer has o'er-brimm'd their clammy cells.

Who hath not seen thee oft amid thy store?
   Sometimes whoever seeks abroad may find
Thee sitting careless on a granary floor,
   Thy hair soft-lifted by the winnowing wind;
Or on a half-reap'd furrow sound asleep,
   Drows'd with the fume of poppies, while thy hook
     Spares the next swath and all its twined flowers,
   And sometimes like a gleaner thou dost keep
Steady thy laden head across a brook;
Or by a cider-press, with patient look,
     Thou watchest the last oozings hours by hours.

Where are the songs of Spring? Ay, where are they?
   Think not of them, thou hast thy music too,—
While barred clouds bloom the soft-dying day;
   And touch the stubble-plains with rosy hue;
Then in a wailful choir the small gnats mourn
   Among the river sallows, borne aloft
     Or sinking as the light wind lives or dies;
   And full-grown lambs loud bleat from hilly bourn;
Hedge-crickets sing; and now with treble soft
The redbreast whistles from a garden-croft,
     And gathering swallows twitter in the skies.

JOHN KEATS

Much could be said about this poem in a general way:
continually concerned with the problem of thought and

sensation, Keats did not always succeed in fusing the two. Sometimes, as in *Ode on a Grecian Urn*, the thought seems to be tacked on at the end of a very beautiful descriptive passage, rather than grow out of it. In the ode *To Autumn*, however, description and thought are one. Mind and senses are united. The whole poem is a celebration of the harvest, a hymn of praise of fruition; its keynote is one of tranquil fulfilment. The tone of the third stanza is, indeed, unmistakably sad, but it is the sadness of resignation, of acceptance, not that of despair and frustration.

The construction of the poem is simple: it consists of three separate, yet related, evocations of autumn—the first through the senses of sight and taste; the second through those of sight and smell; the third through that of hearing.

The first stanza draws a peaceful picture of the English countryside laden with ripe and swelling fruit and mellow with honey; the second begins with an apostrophe to a personified autumn, which is then represented as an allegorical figure now on the threshing-floor, now in a half-reaped cornfield, now as a gleaner, and finally at a cider-making. There is perhaps no other poem which more perfectly evokes the sight and smell of harvest in all its languid warmth and fullness.

In the final stanza, after a fleeting reference to 'the songs of spring', and a marvellous picture of the stubble-fields at sunset (a picture which we know, from one of Keats's letters, to have been drawn directly from observation), we hear the 'wailful choir' of gnats and the varying sounds of the lamb, the cricket, the robin and the swallows. Not only does the third stanza round off the poem with this manifold appeal to the ear (perhaps the least sensual of the senses), it evokes the sad yet tranquil atmosphere of evening. The first stanza may perhaps suggest morning, with its reference to the sun and to buds; the second certainly suggests the heat of the day; and the third suggests the cool of evening which brings the day to a close. This further strengthens the unity of the poem.

The versification is smooth without monotony, the verbal 'music' is exquisite. The magic by which this enhances the pictorial and other imagery and expresses the harmony and contentment of the poet's mood, is beyond analysis.

13

QUOTATION

43

The Cool Web

Children are dumb to say how hot the day is,
How hot the scent is of the summer rose,
How dreadful the black wastes of evening sky,
How dreadful the tall soldiers drumming by.

But we have speech, to chill the angry day,
And speech, to dull the rose's cruel scent.
We spell away the overhanging night,
We spell away the soldiers and the fright.

There's a cool web of language winds us in,
Retreat from too much joy or too much fear:
We grow sea-green at last and coldly die
In brininess and volubility.

But if we let our tongues lose self-possession,
Throwing off language and its watery clasp
Before our death, instead of when death comes,
Facing the wide glare of the children's day,
Facing the rose, the dark sky and the drums,
We shall go mad no doubt and die that way.

ROBERT GRAVES

Among living poets Robert Graves is one whose uncommon richness of imagery suggests that his senses are, so to speak, very near the surface: he thinks in images; an image is always ready to hand to illustrate, illuminate, or symbolize an idea.

The Cool Web is written in a variation on a traditional form. The iambic pentameters are regular without being mechanical; the rhyme-scheme (*abcc*, except in the last verse) is unusual. The language and the thought are on the whole simple: the impression left in the mind by the images is strong. The impression of heat, noise and fear may remain in some readers' minds after they have forgotten the thought of the poem. Yet the thought is original and worth studying.

It is, briefly, that adults employ language as a means of protection against the power of raw feeling as experienced by children. We deliberately blunt our sensibilities in order to prevent them from maddening us.

In the first verse 'Children are dumb', we are told, to express their feelings—four examples are given of the sort of impression that affects children strongly: the heat of the day, the smell of a rose, the darkness of evening, and the noise of soldiers marching past with drums. In verses 2 and 3 the idea is developed that adults use language to protect themselves against excessive sensibility. Language is a cool, watery web which wraps us round, so that in the end we die of too much water and too many words. Finally, if we were to throw off the watery clasp of language and accept experience, as a child receives it, with all the shock of its original impact, no doubt it would drive us mad and kill us.

Graves takes the argument no further: indeed, he is not primarily concerned with arguing. He simply states the discovery about the effect of growing up on experience, using for his purpose the most striking imagery he can draw from recollections of childhood. He might have gone on to say that the poet is he who preserves the strength of childhood sensibility without going mad, and his poems are the result. But he is content to state the discovery and ignore further implications.

QUOTATION

44

The Haunted House

'Come, surly fellow, come: a song!'
    What, fools? Sing to you?
Choose from the clouded tales of wrong
    And terror I bring to you:

Of a night so torn with cries,
    Honest men sleeping
Start awake with rabid eyes,
    Bone-chilled, flesh creeping,

Of spirits in the web-hung room
    Up above the stable,
Groans, knockings in the gloom,
    The dancing table,

Of demons in the dry well
    That cheep and mutter,
Clanging of an unseen bell,
    Blood choking the gutter,

Of lust filthy past belief
    Lurking unforgotten,
Unrestrainable endless grief
    In breasts long rotten.

A song? What laughter or what song
    Can this house remember?
Do flowers and butterflies belong
    To a blind December?

ROBERT GRAVES

In *The Haunted House* thought is again expressed by implication through concrete and striking imagery. In the first line an unnamed 'surly fellow' is ordered to sing. The rest of the poem is an expostulation by the singer against singing in a haunted house—

> A song? What laughter or what song
>   Can this house remember?
> Do flowers and butterflies belong
>   To a blind December?

All the central verses of the poem are taken up with enumerating the various horrors by which the house is haunted, and which make healthy laughter and song impossible—night-cries, spirits, groans, knockings, demons, and other bloody and disgusting terrors. It is right that these things should be dwelt on, for it is they which possess the mind of the speaker and make it impossible for him to think of normal and happy 'song'.

We could well leave the poem there, but it is obvious, if we are familiar with Graves's poems, that the real meaning lies deeper. For the 'surly fellow' and his 'song' must be the poet and the poems that are expected of him; the haunted house is his mind—a mind temporarily obsessed with horror to the exclusion of laughter and happiness.

QUOTATION
45

> *'I Look into my Glass'*
>
> I look into my glass,
> And view my wasting skin,
> And say, 'Would God it came to pass
> My heart had shrunk as thin!'

For then, I undistrest
By hearts grown cold to me,
Could lonely wait my endless rest
With equanimity.

But Time, to make me grieve,
Part steals, lets part abide:
And shakes this fragile frame at eve
With throbbings of noontide.

THOMAS HARDY

Graves is a poet of strong and trenchant imagery and well-marked rhythms. Hardy's poems present a much quieter picture; his imagery is not rich and is as a rule homely; his rhythms are more tentative; his diction is often queer and stiff, a mixture of homely phrases and literary, almost donnish, words; he strikes us as a shy voice, somewhat intimate, sometimes asking for pity, sometimes even querulous. In this poem, as in many others, he faces the facts of his destiny calmly, honestly, and without hysteria or histrionics.

At first sight it appears to have nothing in common with either of the poems by Robert Graves. The imagery is not strong in sense-impressions. We can see an old man looking at his wrinkles in a mirror: for the rest, we have to share his musings on 'hearts grown cold', his 'lonely rest', time that steals, and a 'fragile frame' shaken with 'throbbings of noontide'. There is nothing here to make strong impact on the senses. Yet if we follow the argument, we shall see that like *The Cool Web* it too is concerned with poetic sensibility, passionate feelings that trouble the old man as they once troubled the dumb children of Graves's poem.

In verse 1 Hardy breaks into a cry of regret that his heart has not shrunk as his body has. For then, he says in verse 2, he could await his death with resignation, undistressed by the indifference or death of those who once loved him. But he says finally, as if to grieve him, time steals his youth but leaves him the passionate feelings of youth, so that in the evening of life his frail body is shaken with feeling as it was in life's noontide.

In this pathetic self-revelation Hardy would have sacrificed the reader's sympathy if he had not written with simplicity and sincerity, if he had expressed his self-pity in more downright terms or ranted in heroic vein about the agonies of old age. As it is, the poem is deeply moving.

14

QUOTATION
46

First Love

I ne'er was struck before that hour
 With love so sudden and so sweet.
Her face it bloomed like a sweet flower
 And stole my heart away complete.
My face turned pale as deadly pale,
 My legs refused to walk away,
And when she looked 'what could I ail?'
 My life and all seemed turned to clay.

And then my blood rushed to my face
 And took my sight away.
The trees and bushes round the place
 Seemed midnight at noonday.
I could not see a single thing,
 Words from my eyes did start;
They spoke as chords do from the string
 And blood burnt round my heart.

Are flowers the winter's choice?
    Is love's bed always snow?
She seemed to hear my silent voice
    And love's appeal to know.
I never saw so sweet a face
    As that I stood before:
My heart has left its dwelling-place
    And can return no more.

                                        JOHN CLARE

Earlier in this chapter reference has been made to John Clare, an almost uneducated labourer from a Northamptonshire village whose ruling passion, throughout life, was poetry. He was a man of the countryside, living among the poorest villagers, intimate with rural nature, and writing, like Wordsworth's idealized poet, in 'a selection of the language really used by men'. Like the child in Robert Graves's poem *The Cool Web*, Clare was a man of extreme sensibility, acutely aware of his surroundings and rendered almost helpless by emotion. He was not, like the child, dumb; his feelings burst out into spontaneous poetry.

Now we cannot expect spontaneous poetry to be technically excellent. *Kubla Khan*, if we accept Coleridge's account of its origin, is a brilliant exception. We expect it, above all, to express pure emotion, free from artistic 'working up' and revision; we expect it to be alive with feeling; when the writer is ill-educated, as Clare was, and scarcely literate except in verse, we can expect simplicity, directness, and truth. These are the characteristics of *First Love*.

Clare's aim is to give as truthful a statement of his feelings as possible on first falling in love. In verse 1 he uses the image of a flower to express the effect that the face of the girl had upon him; he goes on to describe the sense of paralysis that her beauty caused him. Verse 2 tells of a feeling almost of suffocation and blindness.

> I could not see a single thing,
> Words from my heart did start.

The meaning of this statement is plain; the form of it is original and surprising. It is referred to again in verse 3:

> She seemed to hear my silent voice
> And love's appeal to know.

The silent voice is the appeal that has come from his blinded eyes. The best he can do to express the sense of this silent appeal is the riddle:

> Are flowers the winter's choice?
> Is love's bed always snow?

The lines are metrically defective, and obviously unrevised; their composition was apparently inspired—Clare could not have worked out logically what he was saying. Winter is the time for snow, love's bed the place for flowers. Must these positions be reversed? he asks. Must love be unfulfilled like flowers born to waste in winter? After this, the remaining four lines seem somewhat trite, and they do not follow inevitably from what precedes them. Technically it is a far from perfect poem; it has flaws of structure and diction, but not of taste or feeling. It needs revision. The title does not seem to have been fully considered; what Clare means is perhaps Love at First Sight, not First Love. Yet we cannot doubt the essential truth of the poem. It describes with almost unequalled closeness an emotion—a psychological incident almost impossible to describe without sentimentality or false touches. It bears out Wordsworth's belief that those most closely in touch with nature experience emotion more purely and intensely than those in a more sophisticated way of life.

Love, poetry, and nature composed almost the whole of Clare's existence. There never was a poet more intimate with nature; he remained her rapturous adorer all his life. To him the music which was assured of immortality was not the songs of men, the sound of human voices, or words in books; it was the music of nature. This is not an original thought; it is not, in itself, a profound thought. It is scarcely a thought at all. As expressed in *Song's Eternity* it is an instinctive conviction arising from an intimate knowledge of, and never-failing delight in, the songs of the birds. For all the boldness of its assertion, the poem is unpretentious, persuasive, and full of grace and tenderness.

QUOTATION

47

Song's Eternity

What is song's eternity?
    Come and see.
Can it noise and bustle be?
    Come and see.
Praises sung or praises said
    Can it be?
Wait awhile and these are dead—
    Sigh, sigh;
Be they high or lowly bred
    They die.

What is song's eternity?
    Come and see.
Melodies of earth and sky,
    Here they be.
Song once sung to Adam's ears
    Can it be?

Ballads of six thousand years
   Thrive, thrive;
Songs awakened with the spheres
   Alive.

Mighty songs that miss decay,
   What are they?
Crowds and cities pass away
   Like a day.
Books are writ and books are read;
   What are they?
Years will lay them with the dead—
   Sigh, sigh;
Trifles unto nothing wed.
   They die.

Dreamers, list the honey-bee;
   Mark the tree
Where the bluecap, 'tootle tee,'
   Sings a glee
Sung to Adam and to Eve—
   Here they be.
When floods covered every bough,
   Noah's ark
Heard that ballad singing now;
   Hark, hark,

'Tootle tootle tootle tee'—
   Can it be
Pride and fame must shadows be?
   Come and see—
Every season owns her own;
   Bird and bee
Sing creation's music on;
   Nature's glee
Is in every mood and tone
   Eternity.

The eternity of song
   Liveth here;
Nature's universal tongue
   Singeth here
Songs I've heard and felt and seen
   Everywhere;
Songs like the grass are evergreen:
   The giver
Said 'Live and be'—and they have been,
   For ever.

JOHN CLARE

The poem is diffuse and repetitive; Clare never achieves compression; he did not aim at it. But he has a true instinct for poetic form—that is, for making the pattern of the poem, however loosely it is woven, appropriate to the mood. The short lines give an air of wistful sadness, yet with a hint of playfulness which prevents any temptation to treat the theme too solemnly. In comparison, I cannot help finding Keats's manner showy and rhetorical:

Thou wast not born for death, immortal bird;
   No hungry generations tread thee down.

But it would be irrelevant to press the comparison. Clare's short lines might easily have become disjointed; it was perhaps on this account that he devised the interlocking rhyme-pattern, whose subtlety might at first escape notice.

The music which will live is not that made by men amid the bustle of crowded cities; this will pass away. The songs of earth and sky, the music of the bluecap (a local variant of 'blue tit'), as it was heard in the garden of Eden and in Noah's ark—this is the truly immortal music. There is no need to analyse the argument in detail. It is given very clearly. A word should, however, be said about the line 'Tootle tootle

tootle tee', which is bound to arouse varying responses in different readers. It is a striking line, and is likely to be remembered, even by readers who do not like it, after many other lines are forgotten. To some it is bound to appear absurd, trivial, bathetic. But to others it will appear a stroke of genius; and surely it gives a touch of homeliness and utter simplicity which is quite deliberate on Clare's part. It is as if he were saying, 'Yes, a bird's song is absurd, but I love its very absurdity; how much sweeter to me is its imperturbable and artless monotony than all the contrived and sophisticated songs of civilized men. How miraculous that the Giver should have chosen such music to have lasted from the time of the Flood, the Garden of Eden, the Creation itself.' It is a bold and simple stroke—bold because it risks making the whole atmosphere of the poem ridiculous; simple—what could be simpler? Such strokes are one of the signs of genius.

15

In this chapter a number of poems have been examined closely with the idea of finding out what poetic virtue consists in. We might sum up the result as follows: sincerity and depth of feeling; the expression of the poet's individuality; a continuous feeling for aptness and beauty of language; a vivid sense of concrete objects as metaphors, similes, and symbols for the expression of experience. But of course the real essence of a good poem is indefinable. In approaching a new poem, it is easiest to think of it as being like making the acquaintance of a stranger. If we are at first attracted by the superficial qualities of appearance, manner, speech and so on, we shall wish to go deeper and try to find out what is the essential individuality, the personality of the stranger. We may find that we have been deceived; or we may wish to get to know him still better. We may find him out of our depth, or of no deep interest to us at all. It is as easy to be deceived by a poem as by a person. Only experience can in the long run help us.

Every person is different, whatever outward resemblance he may show to others. Every poem is different, and needs a different approach. Some people are so conventional as to show little real difference between them and their fellows; some poems are mere copies of established forms and ideas. There are hundreds of Elizabethan songs and sonnets, Cavalier lyrics, and eighteenth-century odes which are mere exercises in a fashionable style. Only knowledge can tell us which are genuine and original, and which second-hand.

The right attitude to authority is one of the difficulties of forming a critical judgement. The experts, those who have given much time to the study of literature, can help us in a broad, general way, by indicating what kinds of literature are worth close attention and what kinds are worthless. But our attitude to so-called authority should be sceptical. Even if an expert is right, if his judgement does not help us personally and chime with our own taste, we should at any rate for the time being ignore him. The critic who illuminates a piece of prose or a poem, who makes us see something we did not see before and now find worth seeing—this is the critic we should study and consider.

But there has been no space in this book to consider the judgements of the critics. It has aimed at forming the reader's own judgement—or rather, in showing him how this can be done. Very few poems have been studied in this chapter, which clearly might have gone on almost indefinitely. We have discussed form and content, style, metre, diction, metaphor, irony, didacticism, the sonnet form, and a number of other things which are likely to recur in all practical criticism.

The poems considered have all been short. The principles

which underlie the criticism of longer poems are the same. Such forms as the ballad, the long narrative poem, the ode, and the epic can be, and should be, studied elsewhere. Verse satire has scarcely been touched on; the same is true of light verse, folk-poetry and other forms, not all by any means unimportant. To have considered these matters would have been outside the scope of this book; there are in existence handbooks and histories of literature where the facts can be studied. Here we have aimed rather at the close examination of prose and poetry, together with some study of the critical principles which underlie it. There is no substitute for the continuous application of intelligence, taste and common sense. Provided we take no poem on trust simply because it is popular or appears frequently in anthologies, we should not find it difficult to detect the faults in poems. The first thing to do is to find out exactly *what* a poet says, then consider how he says it; as we proceed, we shall find that our judgement as to whether it is worth saying tends to form itself automatically. Let us take one or two isolated examples. Wordsworth's famous poem *The Solitary Reaper* appears on examination to be defective, at any rate at the beginning.

> Behold her, *single* in the field,
>   Yon *solitary* Highland lass,
> Reaping and singing *by herself*;
>   Stop here, or gently pass!
> *Alone* she cuts and binds the grain . . .

There is really no earthly reason for telling us in four different ways that she is by herself; nor does the phrase 'in the field' tell us much, since it is stressed elsewhere that she is reaping, and this is the obvious place in which to reap. It is clear that Wordsworth is padding. Hymns and carols are a fairly common source of feeble verse, because the hymn-writer is under the necessity of filling out his material to fit a given tune. The second line of 'While shepherds watched their flocks by night' has always seemed to me a weak line. And how many singers of *Good King Wenceslas* have paused to wonder why an old man comes 'a good league' through heavy snow to gather winter fuel when he lives 'right against the forest fence'? But it is easy to pick holes in poor verse. It is much more important and valuable to form our opinions of what constitutes *good* verse. That is the surest, and in the end the only, way to prevent ourselves from wasting time on what is worthless. It is well to remember that in the world of poetry, as in the world of men, however much our minds hanker after absolute judgements and infallible standards, there will always be differences of taste and opinion. The best that we can hope to agree on is whether or not a particular poem is good of its kind. If we do not happen to like its kind, we need not trouble ourselves unduly. It is no use disliking a poem merely because somebody has proved infallibly that it is bad, unless we are thereby enabled to appreciate better something else which is good.

Rhetorical and showy verse is always something to be regarded with suspicion. Byron's famous address to the sea has long had many admirers.

> Roll on, thou deep and dark blue Ocean—roll!
> Ten thousand fleets sweep over thee in vain;
> Man marks the earth with ruin—his control
>   Stops with the shore.

This is an empty and ridiculous thought: fleets do not sweep over the ocean in vain, because their purpose is not to mark the face of the water. True, man marks the earth with ruin, but he also marks it with useful cultivation. His achievement in making use of both the sea and the land is considerable.

Nevertheless, as a general evocation of crude feelings about the littleness of man in comparison with the immensity of the ocean, the lines may be considered effective. But not all rhetoric is empty. Faustus's lines to Helen are high rhetoric.

> Was this the face that launched a thousand ships,
> And burnt the topless towers of Ilium?
> Sweet Helen, make me immortal with a kiss!

But, hyperbolical as they are, they are more moving because they evoke in a compressed form the whole pity and tragedy of the Trojan War and the sense of wonder aroused by ideal beauty. It is true that Helen's face launched a thousand ships in a sense in which it is not true that 'ten thousand fleets sweep over thee in vain'.

But of course it is always possible that one is affected in one's judgement by a general preference for Marlowe over Byron.

The problem of how far personal bias must affect critical judgement is perhaps insoluble; but the more deeply and thoroughly one trains the critical judgement, the less dependent will it be on personal prejudice and the influence of fashion; and the truer and deeper will be our appreciation of literature.

POEMS FOR CRITICISM

(Names of authors given at end of Chapter, page 147)

1

Snow

Ridged thickly on black bough
  And foaming on twig-fork in swollen lumps
At flirt of bird-wing or wind's sough
  Plump snow tumbled on snow softly with sudden dumps.

Where early steps had made
   A wavering track through the white-blotted road
Breaking its brightness with blue shade
   Snow creaked beneath my feet with snow heavily shod.

I reached a snow-thatched rick
   Where men sawed bedding off for horse and cow;
There varnished straws were lying thick
   Paving with streaky gold the trodden silver snow.

Such light filled me with awe
   And nothing marred my paradisal thought,
That robin least of all I saw
   Lying too fast asleep, his song choked in his throat.

2

Criticize the following poems, translated from the Chinese, discussing whether or not they are sentimental.

(a)   *The Big Rug*

That so many of the poor should suffer from cold what can
    we do to prevent?
To bring warmth to a single body is not much use.
I wish I had a big rug ten thousand feet long,
Which at one time could cover up every inch of the City.

(b)   *A Love Song*

   I heard my love was going to Yang-chou
   And went with him as far as Ch'u-shan.
   For a moment when you held me fast in your
      outstretched arms
   I thought the river stood still and did not flow.

3
Dulce et decorum est

Bent double, like old beggars under sacks,
Knock-kneed, coughing like hags, we cursed through sludge,
Till on the haunting flares we turned our backs,
And towards our distant rest began to trudge.
Men marched asleep. Many had lost their boots,
But limped on, blood-shod. All went lame, all blind;
Drunk with fatigue; deaf even to the hoots
Of gas-shells dropping dropping softly behind.

Gas! GAS! Quick, boys!—An ecstasy of fumbling,
Fitting the clumsy helmets just in time,
But someone still was yelling out and stumbling
And floundering like a man in fire or lime.—
Dim through the misty panes and thick green light,
As under a green sea, I saw him drowning.

In all my dreams before my helpless sight
He plunges at me, guttering, choking, drowning.

If in some smothering dreams, you too could pace
Behind the wagon that we flung him in,
And watch the white eyes writhing in his face,
His hanging face, like a devil's sick of sin;
If you could hear, at every jolt, the blood
Come gargling from the froth-corrupted lungs,
Bitter as the cud
Of vile, incurable sores on innocent tongues,—
My friend, you would not tell with such high zest
To children ardent for some desperate glory,
The old Lie: Dulce et decorum est
Pro patria mori.

4

Compare the treatment of similar subjects in the following three poems.

(a)   *On a Fly Drinking out of his Cup*

Busy, curious, thirsty fly!
Drink with me and drink as I:
Freely welcome to my cup,
Couldst thou sip and sip it up:
Make the most of life you may,
Life is short and wears away.

Both alike are mine and thine
Hastening quick to their decline:
Thine's a summer, mine's no more,
Though repeated to three score.
Three score summers, when they're gone,
Will appear as short as one!

(b)   *House or Window Flies*

These little indoor dwellers, in cottages and halls, were always entertaining me; after dancing in the window all day from sunrise to sunset they would sip of the tea, drink of the beer, and eat of the sugar, and be welcome all summer long. They look like things of mind or fairies, and seem pleased or dull as the weather permits. In many clean cottages and genteel houses, they are allowed every liberty to creep, fly, or do as they like; and seldom or ever do wrong. In fact they are the small or dwarfish portion of our own family, and so many fairy familiars that we know and treat as one of ourselves.

(c)   *An August Midnight*

A shaded lamp and a waving blind,
And the beat of a clock from a distant floor:
On this scene enter—winged, horned, and spined—

A longlegs, a moth, and a dumbledore*;
While 'mid my page there idly stands
A sleepy fly, that rubs its hands . . .

Thus meet we five, in this still place,
At this point of time, at this point in space.
—My guests besmear my new-penned line,
Or bang at the lamp and fall supine.
'God's humblest, they!' I muse. Yet why?
They know Earth-secrets that know not I.

* Cockchafer.

5

Strange fits of passion have I known:
And I will dare to tell,
But in the lover's ear alone,
What once to me befell.

When she I loved looked every day
Fresh as a rose in June,
I to her cottage bent my way,
Beneath an evening-moon.

Upon the moon I fixed my eye,
All over the wide lea;
With quickening pace my horse drew nigh
Those paths so dear to me.

And now we reached the orchard-plot;
And, as we climbed the hill,
The sinking moon to Lucy's cot
Came near, and nearer still.

In one of those sweet dreams I slept,
Kind Nature's gentlest boon!

And all the while my eyes I kept
On the descending moon.

My horse moved on; hoof after hoof
He raised, and never stopped:
When down behind the cottage roof,
At once, the bright moon dropped.

What fond and wayward thoughts will slide
Into a Lover's head!
'O mercy!' to myself I cried,
'If Lucy should be dead!'

6

Invictus

Out of the night that covers me,
  Black as the pit from pole to pole,
I thank whatever Gods may be
  For my unconquerable soul.

In the fell clutch of circumstance
  I have not winced nor cried aloud.
Under the bludgeonings of chance
  My head is bloody but unbowed.

Beyond this place of wrath and tears
  Looms but the horror of the shade,
And yet the menace of the years
  Finds and shall find me unafraid.

It matters not how strait the gate,
  How charged with punishments the scroll,
I am the master of my fate:
  I am the captain of my soul.

7
Another Spring

How beautiful the country now
With blossom white upon the bough,
As slowly through the ocean sky
The clouds like sailing-ships ride by.

A ploughman goes with steady tread
Across the field, the russet red
Of earth shines golden in the light,
Gashed by the lapwings' black and white.

Though many Springs have come and passed
Each seems more lovely than the last;
But when for me all Springs are done
And darkness shuts out sky and sun. . . .

Others will marvel how each year
The miracles of Spring appear,
And with my eyes will find delight
In blossom, sky and lapwings' flight.
    Easter 1949

8
London Snow

When men were all asleep the snow came flying,
  In large white flakes falling on the city brown,
Stealthily and perpetually settling and loosely lying,
  Hushing the latest traffic of the drowsy town;
Deadening, muffling, stifling its murmurs failing;
Lazily and incessantly floating down and down:
  Silently sifting and veiling road, roof and railing;
Hiding difference, making unevenness even,
Into angles and crevices softly drifting and sailing.
  All night it fell, and when full inches seven
It lay in the depth of its uncompacted lightness,

The clouds blew off from a high and frosty heaven;
  And all woke earlier for the unaccustomed brightness
Of the winter dawning, the strange unheavenly glare:
The eye marvelled—marvelled at the dazzling whiteness;
  The ear harkened to the stillness of the solemn air;
No sound of wheel rumbling nor of foot falling,
And the busy morning cries came thin and spare.

  Then boys I heard, as they went to school, calling,
They gathered up the crystal manna to freeze
Their tongues with tasting, their hands with snowballing;
  Or rioted in a drift, plunging up to the knees;
Or peering up from under the white-mossed wonder,
'O look at the trees!' they cried, 'O look at the trees!'

  With lessened load a few carts creak and blunder,
Following along the white deserted way,
A country company long dispersed asunder:
  When now already the sun, in pale display
Standing by Paul's high dome, spread forth below
His sparkling beams, and awoke the stir of the day.

  For now doors open, and war is waged with the snow;
And trains of sombre men, past tale of number,
Tread long brown paths, as toward their toil they go:
  But even for them awhile no cares encumber
Their minds diverted; the daily word is unspoken,
The daily thoughts of labour and sorrow slumber
At the sight of the beauty that greets them, for the
    charm they have broken.

9

Compare the following two poems, which deal with a single
theme in different styles.

(a)   *Description of Spring*
              Wherein each thing renews save only the lover
    The sweet season that bud and bloom forth brings,
    With green hath clad the hill and eke the vale:

The nightingale with feathers new she sings:
The turtle to her make* hath told her tale:
Summer is come, for every spray now springs,
The hart hath hung his old head on the pale:
The buck in brake his winter coat he flings:
The fishes float with new-repairèd scale:
The adder all her slough away she slings:
The swift swallow pursueth the fliès small:
The busy bee her honey now she mings†:
Winter is worn that was the flowers bale:
And thus I see among these pleasant things
Each care decays, and yet my sorrow springs.

      * sweetheart.   † remembers.

(*b*)

Now fades the last long streak of snow,
  Now burgeons every maze of quick
  About the flowering squares, and thick
By ashen roots the violets blow.

Now rings the woodland loud and long,
  The distance takes a lovelier hue,
  And drown'd in yonder living blue
The lark becomes a sightless song.

Now dance the lights on lawn and lea,
  The flocks are whiter down the vale,
  And milkier every milky sail
On winding stream or distant sea;

Where now the seamew pipes or dives
  In yonder greening gleam, and fly
  The happy birds that change their sky
To build and brood; that live their lives

From land to land; and in my breast
   Spring wakens too; and my regret
   Becomes an April violet,
And buds and blossoms like the rest.

10

Sea-Distances

Above the purple heather, the pasture of the bee,
A summer cloud came softly, as a swan from the sea,
And bright and clear below me, a mile or so away,
A sail like the Windflower was beating up the bay.

Could I have come aboard her, as if there had not been
The long years of havoc, the bitter years between,
My old friend would be steering, and I should find
   him there,
With a line out for mackerel, and a line perhaps to spare.

A fair sky above him, the flowing wave beneath,
A head-wind to master, and a pipe between his teeth,
His hand on the tiller, and his finger on the line,
There'd be creels of blue and silver for that old friend
   of mine;

Heaps of quick and slippery silver, all bestreaked with
   green and blue,
And I'd take a turn at steering while he filled his pipe anew,
And he should talk of timeless things and watch the
   changing skies,
With a jest on his lips and the wisdom in his eyes.

O softly flowed the white cloud above that pleasant lea,
But the gray shadows followed and began to dusk the sea.
I could not see the white sail; I could not see the bay;
For my friend and the Windflower were forty years away.

11

The New House

Now first, as I shut the door,
   I was alone
In the new house; and the wind
   Began to moan.

Old at once was the house,
   And I was old;
My ears were teased with the dread
   Of what was foretold,

Nights of storm, days of mist, without end;
   Sad days when the sun
Shone in vain; old griefs and griefs
   Not yet begun.

All was foretold me; nought
   Could I foresee;
But I learned how the wind would sound
   After these things should be.

12

301

this little bride & groom are
standing) in a kind
of crown he dressed
in black candy she

veiled with candy white
carrying a bouquet of
pretend flowers this
candy crown with this candy

little bride & little
groom in it kind of stands on
a thin ring which stands on a much
less thin very much more

big & kinder of ring and which
kinder of stands on a
much more than very much
biggest & thickest & kindest

of ring & all one two three rings
are cake & everything is protected by
cellophane against anything (because
nothing really exists

13

An Old Man Playing with Children

A discreet householder exclaims on the grandsire
In war paint and feathers, with fierce grandsons and axes
Dancing round a backyard fire of boxes:
'Watch grandfather, he'll set the house on fire.'

But I will unriddle for you the thought of his mind,
An old one you cannot open with conversation.
What animates the thin legs in risky motion?
Mixes the snow on the head with snow on the wind?

'Grandson, grandsire. We are equally boy and boy.
Do not offer your reclining-chair and slippers
With tedious old women talking in wrappers.
This life is not good but in danger and in joy.

'It is you the elder to these and younger to me
Who are penned as slaves by properties and causes
And never walk from your shaped insupportable houses
And shamefully, when boys shout, go in and flee.

'May God forgive me, I know your middling ways,
Having taken care and performed ignominies unreckoned
Between the first brief childhood and the brief second,
But I will be the more honourable in these days.'

14
Last Love-word

This is the last; the very, very last!
　　Anon, and all is dead and dumb,
Only a pale shroud over the past,
　　　That cannot be
　　Of value small or vast,
　　　Love, then to me!

I can say no more; I have even said too much.
　　I did not mean that this should come:
　　I did not know 'twould swell to such—
　　　Nor, perhaps, you—
　　When that first look and touch,
　　　Love, doomed us two!

15
Meet we no Angels, Pansie?*

Came, on a Sabbath noon, my sweet,
　　In white, to find her lover;
The grass grew proud beneath her feet,
　　The green elm-leaves above her:—
　　Meet we no angels, Pansie?

She said, 'We meet no angels now';
　　And soft lights stream'd upon her;

---

* This poem was included in the original editions of *The Oxford Book of English Verse* (1900), but omitted from the revised edition (1939). In criticizing it, comment on this procedure.

And with white hands she touch'd a bough;
  She did it that great honour:—
    What! meet no angels, Pansie?

O sweet brown hat, brown hair, brown eyes,
  Down-dropp'd brown eyes, so tender!
Then what said I? Gallant replies
  Seem flattery, and offend her:—
    But—meet no angels, Pansie?

16

(a)

To a Mouse

On turning her up in her nest with the plough, November 1785

Wee, sleekit, cow'rin', tim'rous beastie,
O what a panic's in thy breastie!
Thou need na start awa saw hasty,
  Wi' bickering brattle!
I wad be laith to rin and chase thee
  Wi' murd'ring pattle!

I'm truly sorry man's dominion
Has broken nature's social union,
An' justifies that ill opinion
  Which makes thee startle
At me, thy poor earth-born companion,
  An' fellow-mortal!

I doubt na, whiles, but thou may thieve;
What then? poor beastie, thou maun live!
A daimen-icker in a thrave
  'S a sma' request:
I'll get a blessin' wi' the lave,
  And never miss't!

Thy wee bit housie, too, in ruin!
It's silly wa's the win's are strewin':
And naething, now, to big a new ane,
    O' foggage green!
An' bleak December's winds ensuin'
   Baith snell and keen!

Thou saw the fields laid bare and waste
An' weary winter comin' fast,
An' cozie here, beneath the blast,
    You thought to dwell,
Till, crash! the cruel coulter past
   Out thro' thy cell.

That wee bit heap o' leaves an' stibble
Has cost thee mony a weary nibble!
Now thou's turned out, for a' thy trouble,
    But house or hald,
To thole the winter's sleety dribble
   An' cranreuch cauld!

But Mousie, thou art no thy lane
In proving foresight may be vain:
The best laid schemes o' mice an' men
    Gang aft a-gley,
An' lea'e us nought but grief an' pain,
   For promised joy.

Still thou art blest, compared wi' me!
The present only toucheth thee:
But, och! I backward cast my e'e
    On prospects drear!
An' forward, tho' I canna see,
   I guess an' fear!

(b)

Mouse's Nest

I found a ball of grass among the hay
And progged it as I passed and went away;
And when I looked I fancied something stirred,
And turned agen and hoped to catch the bird—
When out an old mouse bolted in the wheats
With all her young ones hanging at her teats;
She looked so odd and so grotesque to me,
I ran and wondered what the thing could be,
And pushed the knapweed bunches where I stood;
Then the mouse hurried from the craking brood.
The young ones squeaked, and as I went away
She found her nest again among the hay.
The water o'er the pebbles scarce could run
And broad old cesspools glittered in the sun.

17

To the Evening Star

Thou fair-hair'd angel of the evening,
Now, whilst the sun rests on the mountains, light
Thy bright torch of love; thy radiant crown
Put on, and smile upon our evening bed!
Smile on our loves, and, while thou drawest the
Blue curtains of the sky, scatter thy silver dew
On every flower that shuts its sweet eyes
In timely sleep. Let thy west wind sleep on
The lake; speak silence with thy glimmering eyes,
And wash the dusk with silver. Soon, full soon,
Dost thou withdraw; then the wolf rages wide,
And the lion glares thro' the dun forest:
The fleeces of our flocks are cover'd with
Thy sacred dew: protect them with thine influence.

18

(a)   *Song on May Morning*

Now the bright morning-star, Day's harbinger,
Comes dancing from the east and leads with her
The flowery May, who from her green lap throws
The yellow cowslip and the pale primrose.
  Hail, bounteous May, that dost inspire
  Mirth, and youth, and warm desire!
  Woods and groves are of thy dressing;
  Hill and dale doth boast thy blessing.
Thus we salute thee with our early song,
And welcome thee and wish thee long.

     The year's at the spring
     And day's at the morn;
     Morning's at seven;
     The hill-side's dew-pearled;
     The lark's on the wing;
     The snail's on the thorn:
     God's in his heaven—
     All's right with the world!

19

The Swallow

The morning that my baby came
They found a baby swallow dead,
And saw a something, hard to name,
Flit moth-like over baby's bed.

My joy, my flower, my baby dear
Sleeps on my bosom well, but Oh!
If in the Autumn of the year
When swallows gather round and go——

20

The Sea

It keeps eternal whisperings around
    Desolate shores, and with its mighty swell
    Gluts twice ten thousand caverns, till the spell
Of Hecate leaves them their old shadowy sound.
Often 'tis in such gentle temper found,
    That scarcely will the very smallest shell
    Be moved for days from whence it sometime fell,
When last the winds of heaven were unbound.
Oh ye! who have your eyeballs vexed and tired,
    Feast them upon the wideness of the sea;
      Oh ye! whose ears are dinned with uproar rude,
    Or fed with too much cloying melody—
      Sit ye near some old cavern's mouth and brood
Until ye start, as if the sea-nymphs quired!

AUTHORS OF THE FOREGOING POEMS

1. *Snow:* Andrew Young.
2. (*a*) *The Big Rug,* (*b*) *A Love Song:* Arthur Waley.
3. *Dulce et decorum est:* Wilfred Owen.
4. (*a*) *On a Fly Drinking out of his Cup:* William Oldys.
   (*b*) *House or Window Flies:* John Clare.
   (*c*) *An August Midnight:* Thomas Hardy.
5. *Strange fits of passion:* William Wordsworth.
6. *Invictus:* William Ernest Henley.
7. *Another Spring:* Douglas Gibson.
8. *London Snow:* Robert Bridges.
9. (*a*) *Description of Spring:* Henry Howard, Earl of Surrey.
   (*b*) *Now fades the last long streak of snow:* Alfred Lord Tennyson.
10. *Sea Distances:* Alfred Noyes.
11. *The New House:* Edward Thomas.
12. *301:* E. E. Cummings.
13. *An Old Man Playing with Children:* John Crowe Ransom.

14. *Last Love-word:* Thomas Hardy.
15. *Meet we no Angels, Pansie?* Thomas Ashe.
16. (*a*) *To a Mouse:* Robert Burns.
    (*b*) *Mouse's Nest:* John Clare.
17. *To the Evening Star:* William Blake.
18. (*a*) *Song on May Morning:* John Milton.
    (*b*) *The year's at the spring:* Robert Browning.
19. *The Swallow:* Ralph Hodgson.
20. *The Sea:* John Keats.

GLOSSARY

OF TECHNICAL TERMS AND
LITERARY EXPRESSIONS USED IN THIS BOOK

abstract: of style or diction, without actual or particular examples (as opposed to *concrete*).

alliterative verse: alliteration is the practice of using two or more words beginning with the same letter near together. Alliterative verse is the old English verse form based on this practice, first appearing in Anglo-Saxon times and continuing into the fourteenth century (Langland) and later. It is unrhymed, the lines are loosely dactyllic four-stress lines, containing as a rule two words beginning with the same letter in the first half, and one or two in the second.

antithesis: form of expression, in verse or prose, in which contrasting words emphasize a contrast in ideas (e.g. 'to live a sinner or to die a saint').

apostrophe: direct address to person or idea, usually absent or dead, in course of poem, speech, etc.

appositional phrase: group of words, usually equivalent to a noun, placed beside a noun and having the same grammatical function (e.g. 'Mr. Atkins, *a man of sterling character*, was elected to the vacant office').

archaic: used of word, phrase, style, etc., no longer in ordinary use; old-fashioned or antiquated in flavour.

assonance: near rhyme; similarity of sound without actual rhyme (e.g. 'Full fathom *five* Thy father *lies*').

blank verse: an indefinite number of unrhymed iambic pentameters (see *iambic*, and *pentameter*).

cesura: pause or break in rhythmic flow of a line of verse (e.g. after the second *to be* in 'To be or not to be; that is the question').

clause: group of words consisting of a subject and a predicate. A simple sentence consists of one main clause, a double or multiple sentence contains two or more main clauses. A complex sentence consists of one or more main clauses and one or more dependent or subordinate clauses.

concrete: of style, expression or diction, containing particular examples, as opposed to *abstract* (see above).

dactyl: a foot or measure in verse, consisting of one strong syllable followed by two weak ones (e.g. *fortunate, horribly*).

dependent clause: clause not grammatically independent, but subordinate to another clause. See above, *clause.*

diction: vocabulary, choice of words, especially in poetry. Diction may be simple, homely, learned, pedantic, archaic, colloquial, etc.

didactic: with a propagandist intention, of poetry, fiction, etc. The didactic intention may be moral, social, religious, political, etc. A fable is a short story having a moral purpose, and is therefore didactic.

ellipsis: the shortening of a sentence or phrase by the omission of certain words which can easily be understood from the rest of the sentence or by the reader's common sense (e.g. 'If found, return to Post Office' for 'If this document is found, please return it to the Post Office').

Euphuism: a literary style developed in the Elizabethan period by John Lyly, of which the marks are balance of phrase, excessive alliteration and a systematic use of similes drawn especially from natural history.

finite verb: a verb limited in number, person and tense (e.g. he *loved*, 3rd person singular of the past tense), as opposed to the infinitive (*to love*).

heroic couplet: iambic pentameters rhyming in pairs—*aa bb cc*, etc. Some critics regard all verse written in this form as heroic couplets (e.g. Chaucer's *Prologue*, Keats's *Endymion* and Rupert Brooke's *The Great Lover*). I prefer, with others, to restrict the use of the term to that type of couplet perfected by Pope in the early eighteenth century which, modelled on

Pope's immediate predecessor Dryden, is distinguished by extreme balance and antithesis, so that each couplet is in itself almost an epigram.

hyperbole: a figure of speech in which exaggeration is used deliberately for the sake of emphasis (e.g. Marlowe's 'Is this the face that launched a thousand ships?').

iambic: consisting of a series of iambuses, or relating to the iambus, a measure or foot in verse consisting of one weak syllable followed by one strong one (e.g. repent, at home, connive).

imagery: the images used by a writer of poetry or prose, an image being a picture or other sense-impression conveyed in words. Thus an image in poetry is a word or expression which appeals directly to the eye, the ear, or the senses of taste, touch, and smell. Keats's imagery was strongly sensuous, appealing more often than that of most poets to the sense of taste; Tennyson's imagery appeals often to the ear or the eye, Herrick's imagery often appeals to the sense of touch. Wordsworth's imagery is less rich and vivid than that of some poets, for instance Coleridge, and his appeal is thus less directly to the senses than to the intellect.

inflect: to change the ending of a word to express varying grammatical function. Thus we speak of Latin as a highly inflected language, because the endings of most of its words change according to their grammatical position; French and English are by comparison little inflected.

irony: irony in speech or writing is present wherever the real meaning is to some extent concealed under language of opposite meaning. In its simplest form it is often called sarcasm—'You *are* in a good temper to-day, aren't you?' (meaning exactly the opposite). In its subtler forms it is part of the usual method of highly civilized writers such as Swift, Jane Austen and Thomas Hardy.

lyric: a short song-like poem, often of a musical character, usually in verses or stanzas, expressing directly the poet's thoughts or feelings. The term is used very loosely in English poetic criticism, and is most useful when the writer wishes to distinguish poems of this kind from those in some other form —e.g. epic, narrative or dramatic. Thus, a critic might say he preferred Browning's *lyric* or lyrical poems (meaning *Pippa Passes* or *Home Thoughts from Abroad*) to his philosophical poems (e.g. *Rabbi Ben Ezra* or *Andrea del Sarto*). Blake's lyrical poems are usually considered apart from his long prophetic books. It should be noted, however, that the lyric is not a clearly definable poetic form, like the sonnet: sonnets themselves may very often be classed as lyrics.

metaphor: the application, in prose or poetry, of a word or expression to some other word to which it does not apply literally. There is always an implied, or compressed, comparison. For instance, in Shakespeare's 'There's daggers in men's smiles' (*Macbeth*) the implication is: 'Men conceal enmity beneath their apparent good-will, as a man might conceal a dagger under his cloak'. Here, the original expression has great imaginative force, vividness and compression.

Metaphysicals: the name given to certain English poets of the late sixteenth and seventeenth centuries, notably Donne, Cowley, and in a lesser degree Herbert, Vaughan and Crashaw. The name, first used by Dryden and later adopted by Johnson, referred to their use of far-fetched imagery from intellectual ideas outside the sphere of physical appearances.

octave: the first 8 lines of a sonnet of the Petrarcan type, the remaining 6 lines being the *sestet*. (See below, *sonnet*.)

octosyllabic couplet: an English verse form consisting of a series of four-stressed lines, usually iambic, rhyming in pairs.

onomatopoeia: matching the sound to the sense. Certain words are in themselves of onomatopoeic origin, being attempts to reproduce the sound intended by the word (e.g. splash, fizz, cuckoo). The word also applies to deliberate poetic effects, such as Tennyson's 'The murmur of innumerable bees'. All fully effective poetry is in some degree onomatopoeic, since if the sound did not match the sense, we should consider the lines imperfect. Coleridge's *Kubla Khan*, for instance, is most subtly onomatopoeic throughout, but with no trace of a deliberate seeking after musical effects for their own sake.

paradox: a statement or pair of statements whose meaning is made clear by the reconciliation of apparently irreconcilable ideas (e.g. the proverbial saying 'A short cut is often the longest way round' and the French saying 'Plus ça change, plus c'est la même chose'). The profoundest truths are often concealed in paradoxes, a form favoured by, for instance, Jesus, who often wished to hide his meaning from the ignorant and thoughtless and appeal to those who were prepared to think about truth and try to solve his riddles by reflection and discussion.

participial phrase: a group of words beginning with a present or past participle and grammatically equivalent to an adjective.

pentameter: a line in verse consisting of five feet or measures, and usually iambic in rhythm. See above, *blank verse* and *iambic*.

periphrasis: a roundabout way of saying something. It is sometimes used by a writer as a mild display of vanity or affectation, as when a cook is referred to as 'a practitioner of the culinary art'. In the eighteenth century it was sometimes used to avoid referring directly to inelegant or homely things. It is now considered better style to call a spade a spade, not 'an agricultural implement'.

personification: in prose and especially poetry, referring to an abstract idea or quality as if it were a person. E.g. Gray's *Elegy*:

> Can Honour's voice provoke the silent dust,
> Or Flattery soothe the dull, cold ear of Death?

Renaissance: name given to the general movement in art, literature and thought which began in Italy in the fourteenth century under the influence of a revived interest in Greek and Latin authors, and continued later in France, England, and western Europe generally.

satire: literary or artistic expression whose general aim is to amuse, and sometimes to correct or reform, by means of ridicule.

sentimentality: a somewhat vague expression, not easy to define precisely. Its appearance in prose or poetry can readily be recognized, but in border-line cases critics are often in disagreement about its exact limits. In general, sentimentality usually appears as an *excess* of feeling—the reader feels that the writer is indulging in emotion for its own sake, beyond what the situation demands. For example, extreme regret over something which is past and dead beyond recall might be sentimental.

sestet: see above, *octave*.

simile: a figure of speech in which a comparison is introduced for the sake of added vividness or clarity. E.g. Coleridge, *The Ancient Mariner*:

> Day after day, day after day,
> We stuck, nor breath nor motion;
> *As idle as a painted ship*
> *Upon a painted ocean.*

sonnet: a poem consisting of 14 iambic pentameters rhyming in one of several ways. The two main forms are the Petrarcan, as used mainly after the Elizabethan age by Milton, Wordsworth, Keats and others; and the Shakespearean. The latter consists of three quatrains (four-line verses) followed by a rhymed couplet; the Petrarcan form consists of an octave, followed by a sestet (see above). It avoids the necessity for the final rhymed couplet, which too often reads like an afterthought tagged on at the end.

stanza: another name for a verse in a poem. It consists of a predetermined number of lines, three or more, and most commonly four, usually rhyming in a pattern regularly repeated throughout the poem. Writers such as Keats and Shelley used, especially in their Odes, complex stanza patterns, often adapted from that used by Spenser in *The Faerie Queene*. The word is the same as the Italian word for a 'room'—Donne speaks of 'sonnets' pretty rooms'. The successive stanzas in a poem were though of as being like the rooms in a house, each separate, yet leading out of one another.

tautology: unintentional repetition, saying the same thing more than once in different ways (e.g. 'Alone at last, she stood by herself in the library and meditated in solitude').

BIBLIOGRAPHY

Walter Allen. *Writers on Writing: An Anthology*. (Phoenix House.)

Matthew Arnold. *Essays in Criticism. Second Series*. (Macmillan.)

Owen Barfield. *Poetic Diction*. (Faber.)

F. W. Bateson. *English Poetry: A Critical Introduction*. (Longmans.)

J. Bronowski. *The Poet's Defence*. (Cambridge.)

Cleanthe Brooks and Robert Penn Warren. *Fundamentals of Good Writing*. (Dobson.)

Byron. *English Bards and Scotch Reviewers*. (Collected Poems.)

Bonamy Dobrée. *Modern Prose Style*. (Oxford.)

T. S. Eliot. *Selected Essays*. (Faber.)

E. M. Forster. *Aspects of the Novel*. (Arnold.)

H. W. Fowler. *Modern English Usage*. (Oxford.)

Robert Graves. *The Common Asphodel*. (Hamish Hamilton.)

Robert Graves and Alan Hodge. *The Reader Over Your Shoulder*. (Cape.)

Katherine Hope-Parker. *Language and Reality*. (Muller.)

D. H. Lawrence. *Selected Literary Criticism*. (Heinemann.)

F. R. Leavis. *New Bearings in English Poetry*. (Chatto and Windus.)

C. Day Lewis. *Poetry for You*. (Blackwell.)

John Middleton Murry. *The Problem of Style*. (Oxford.)
John Clare and Other Studies. (Nevill.)

George Orwell. *Critical Essays*. (Secker and Warburg.)

Pope. *Essay on Criticism*. (Collected Poems.)

Herbert Read. *English Prose Style*. (Bell.)

James Reeves. *The Speaking Oak*. (Heinemann.)

I. A. Richards. *Practical Criticism*. (Routledge and Kegan Paul.

Denys Thompson. *Reading and Discrimination*. (Chatto and Windus.)

E. M. W. Tillyard. *Poetry Direct and Oblique*. (Chatto and Windus.)

Edmund Wilson. *Axel's Castle*. (Scribner.)

Raymond Williams. *Reading and Criticism*. (Muller.)

Virginia Woolf. *The Common Reader*, First and Second Series. (Hogarth.)

INDEX TO
PASSAGES QUOTED IN THE TEXT

ACKNOWLEDGEMENTS

The author and publishers wish to thank the following for permission to reprint copyright material:

Messrs Peter Nevill Ltd and Mr J. Middleton Murry for a passage from *John Clare and Other Studies*. Mr Robert Graves and Messrs Hamish Hamilton Ltd for a quotation from *The Common Asphodel*. Sir John Gielgud for a quotation from his Introduction to *The Importance of Being Earnest* (Heinemann). The Oxford University Press for an extract from *The Oxford Junior Encyclopædia*. Mrs Lawrence for an extract from *Lady Chatterley's Lover*. Messrs Alfred A. Knopf for three poems by John Crowe Ransom. Messrs Jonathan Cape Ltd for extracts from *A Portrait of the Artist as a Young Man* by James Joyce; *Babbitt* by Sinclair Lewis; *Arabia Deserta* by Charles Doughty; *Men Without Women* by Ernest Hemingway, and two poems by Andrew Young. The Hogarth Press Ltd for an extract from *To the Lighthouse* by Virginia Woolf. Messrs John Farquharson for an extract from *The Turn of the Screw* by Henry James. Messrs Macmillan & Co. Ltd and the Trustees of the Hardy Estate for extracts from *The Return of the Native* and three poems by Thomas Hardy. Mr Ralph Hodgson and Messrs Macmillan & Co. Ltd for *The Swallow*. Messrs J. M. Dent for an extract from *Green Mansions* by W. H. Hudson. Messrs Chatto & Windus Ltd for extracts from *Swann's Way* by Proust; *On the Margin* by Aldous Huxley: *Huckleberry Finn* by Mark Twain, and a poem by Wilfred Owen. John Lane the Bodley Head Ltd for an extract from *The Good Soldier* by Ford Madox Ford. Mr W. Somerset Maugham for an extract from *The Moon and Sixpence*. Messrs Constable & Co. Ltd for an extract from *The Egoist* by George Meredith; and for *The Big Rug* by Arthur Waley. Messrs George Allen & Unwin Ltd for *A Love Song* by Arthur Waley. Mr Douglas Gibson for *Another Spring* from *The Singing Earth* (Heinemann). The Clarendon Press, Oxford, for *London Snow* from *The Shorter Poems of Robert Bridges*. Mr Alfred Noyes and Messrs William Blackwood & Sons Ltd for *Sea Distances*. Mrs Thomas for two poems by the late Edward Thomas. Mr Robert Graves for his poems *The Cool Web* and *The Haunted House*. The Oxford University Press for an extract from *The Journals of Gerard Manley Hopkins*. Mr E. E. Cummings for three poems. Messrs Faber & Faber Ltd for an extract from *Finnegan's Wake* by James Joyce.